IMAGINING LYND WARD

David A. Beronä

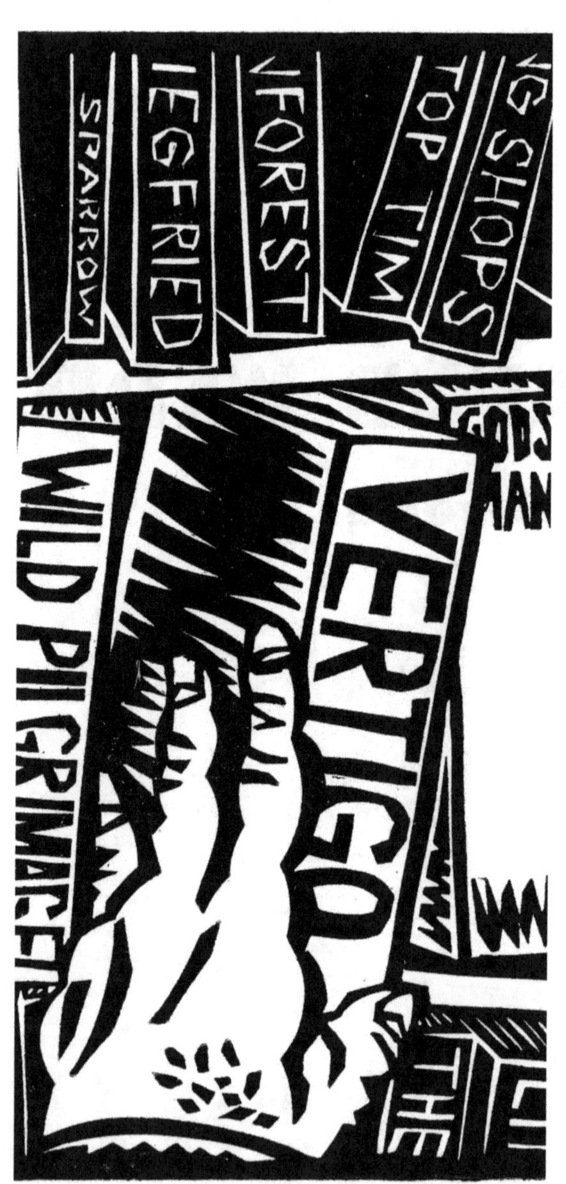
SPARROW
IEGFRIED
VFOREST
TOP TIM
G SHOPS
GODS
MAN
VERTIGO
WILD PILGRIMAGE
THE

IMAGINING LYND WARD

David A. Beronä

Introduction by Eric Drooker

FREEDOM VOICES

Text ©2015 David A. Beronä
Introduction ©2015 Eric Drooker
Images ©2015 Olivier Deprez, Jules Remedios Faye, Drew Grasso, Art Hazelwood, Frances Jetter, Billy Simms, Kurt Brian Webb
The individual works of art reproduced in this collection are copyright by their respective creators and reproduced with permission.

Library of Congress Cataloging-in-Publication Data

Beronä, David A.
Imagining Lynd Ward / David A. Beronä ; Introduction by Eric Drooker.
pages cm
ISBN 978-0-915117-25-3
1. Ward, Lynd, 1905-1985. 2. Wood-engravers--United States--Biography. 3. Novelists, American--20th century--Biography. 4. Graphic novels. I. Drooker, Eric, 1958- writer of introduction. II. Title.
NE1112.W37B47 2015
769.92--dc23
2015025426

Freedom Voices
P.O. Box 423115
San Francisco, CA 94142
www.freedomvoices.org

Design: Art Hazelwood
Editing: Kitty Costello, Maketa Groves, Clifton Ross

Front cover image: Drew Grasso
Frontispiece image: Kurt Brian Webb
Back cover image: Frances Jetter

Imagining Lynd Ward
David A. Beronä

INTRODUCTION

Back in the days before people emailed and texted one another through electronic devices I received a paper envelope in my rusty tenement mailbox from a total stranger. He was eager to discuss my recently-published first book, *Flood! A Novel in Pictures*. In the early 1990s, few people took graphic novels seriously, so I was surprised that a bona fide scholar had written to me requesting an interview.

His name was David A. Beronä, and he was a historian of wordless books–specifically, the woodcut novels that were popular in the 1930s. When he arrived a few weeks later at my Lower East Side studio, he hastily set up a tape recorder and microphone on my kitchen table. Then he began to ask me a series of pointed questions, such as: "Why did you choose to write a book without using any words?" "Who influenced you to be an artist?" "Who inspired you *most*?"

Within the interview's first five minutes, I found myself speaking feverishly about one of my all-time artistic heroes: Lynd Ward.

Q: "When did you first discover his work?"

A: "I'd first seen his work as a child. One day, when I was no more than eleven, my grandfather handed me a strange, dusty book up in his attic. The book had no words in it ... pictures *alone told the entire story.*"

I proceeded to explain how this early encounter with Ward's books led me to produce similar books of my own some years later–books that relied solely on images to weave complex narratives. *Books whose social content was as radical as their wordless form.*

As the tape recorder rolled on, Beronä smiled knowingly. It was obvious that Lynd Ward had made an indelible impression on *him as well. Indeed,* Beronä had long been drawn to Ward's art–and to the handful of other artists who'd attempted wordless storytelling. When Beronä ultimately published his own volume years later, he traced the roots of the form back through history in *Wordless Books: The Original Graphic Novels* (Abrams, 2008).

Apparently, Lynd Ward studied art in Germany as a young man. While he was there he stumbled upon the wordless books of Franz Masereel, a Belgian expressionist known for his political outspokenness and unforgettable, bold woodcuts. Ward had never seen books "written" in pictures before, and Masereel's woodcut novels, created in the 1920s, affected him profoundly. When Ward returned to America, he rolled up his sleeves and vigorously developed the art of wordless storytelling further than anyone yet had.

Of course, the newspaper comic strip had been a popular art form for decades, but it was Ward's long-form narratives that expanded sequential art into a more literary realm; one that dealt with such mature themes as urban alienation, labor unrest, unemployment, corporate greed, spiritual vacuum, repressed sexuality, prostitution, police violence, and suicide. Although Lynd Ward's stories were entertaining and visually stunning, they never allowed the reader to escape into a fantasy world as comics did–but forced the reader to confront reality head on.

Ward created numerous woodcut novels during the years of the Great Depression that were extremely moving and popular with the public. His first book, *God's Man*, was an instant best seller, despite the fact that it was published in October 1929–a week before the stock market crash.

The wordless aspect of Ward's storytelling invited the reader to interpret his silent novels however they wished. Unlike comic strips, Ward had no use for speech balloons, thought bubbles, or captions of any kind. By leaving words out entirely, the experience of "reading" became more interactive and more universal. Woodcut novels transcended the language barrier, and could communicate with anyone, from any culture, despite their tongue, age, or literacy.

So why did Lynd Ward's memorable woodcut novels, that were so popular with the public, go out of style within the next few years?

Talkies.

When sound was added to movies, and the public soon fell under the spell of television, the act of reading wordless books was suddenly passé. By the end of the twentieth century, the books of Lynd Ward were nearly impossible to find anywhere. But just as Ward's work was beginning to slip into cultural oblivion, David A. Beronä began an energetic campaign to remind America about one of its forgotten innovators. He wrote passionately about Lynd Ward's art in various academic journals, *The Comics Journal*–anywhere that would print his essays. Almost singlehandedly, he became impresario to the lost art of wordless storytelling. Thanks to Beronä's tireless advocacy, most of Lynd Ward's novels are once again in print in beautiful new editions, which include new introductions by Beronä himself.

Needless to say, book publishers everywhere now find themselves on a downward spiral, unable to compete with e-books, Kindle, and the Internet. Cultural pundits have placed print media on the endangered species list. *But hold the presses!* The graphic novel is in robust health and is currently one of the few *growing* categories in bookstores. Because of its recent commercial success, sequential art has gained respectability, and the graphic novel is having a renaissance. In the last few years, it has become a more popular and vibrant art form than ever before.

In this bright new era of graphic literacy, many are seriously examining the genealogy of the modern graphic novel. David A. Beronä's historical groundwork is helping a new generation become familiar with the roots of Graphic Storytelling.

Just as the earliest movies were silent, the earliest graphic novels were wordless. If Lynd Ward is the daddy of the graphic novel, Franz Masereel is surely the granddaddy. As a living descendent of these wordless masters, I feel that our unique form of storytelling derives its power from an invisible narrative arc, which unfolds silently in the imagination of our readers. Images resonate on a deeper level than words. Picture-making was the earliest form of writing, and we've been at it for over thirty thousand years.

The extraordinary group of graphic artists whose prints are included in this volume have come together to illustrate a most unusual book by David A. Beronä. In your hands is a rare artifact: A work of historical fiction, and a passionate testament by an art historian–not simply for his love of Lynd Ward's art–but for his love of the artist himself.

Enjoy.

Eric Drooker

Preface

Lynd Interview on Local Cablevision

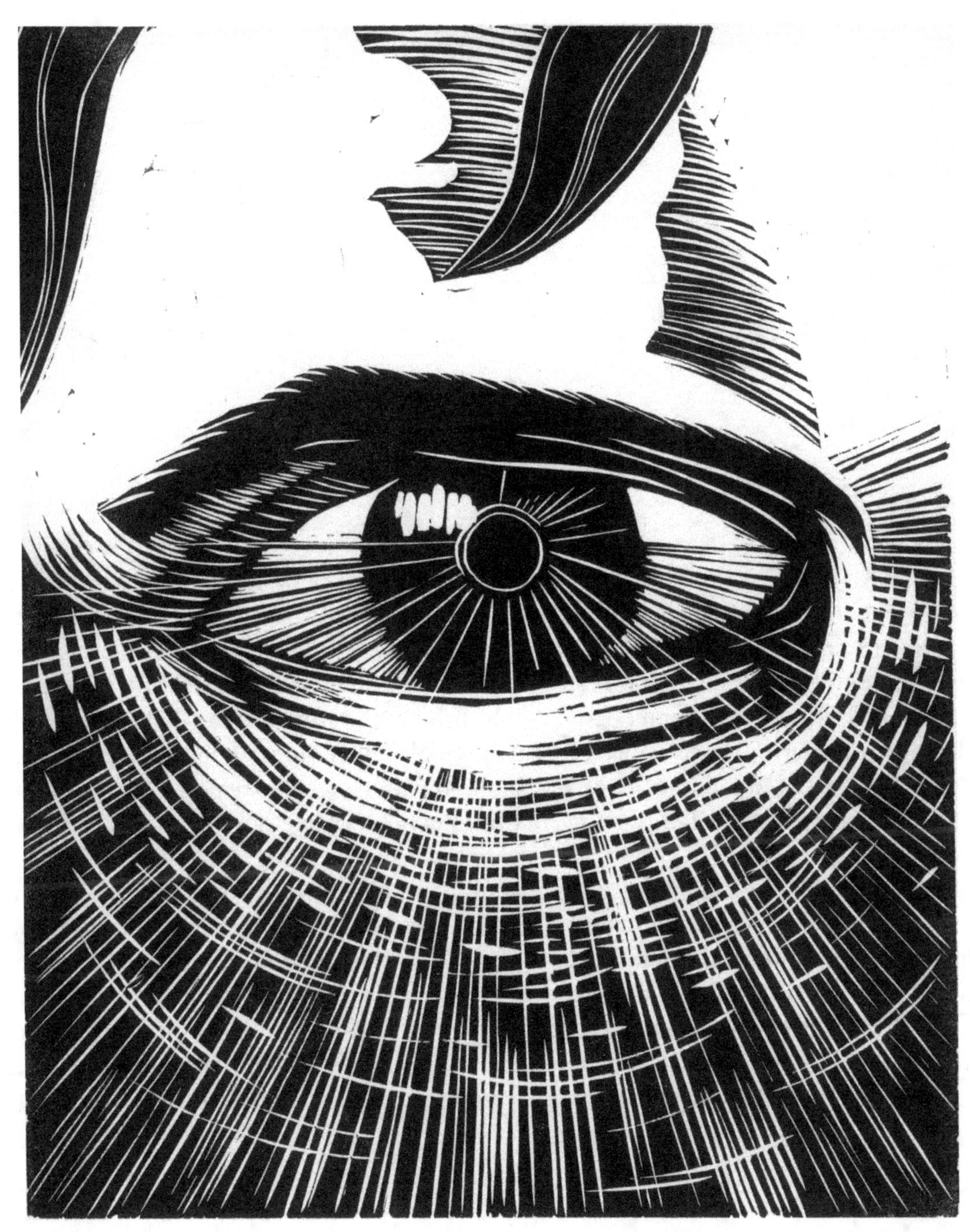

An interview that may have been shown on a local cable station was recorded with Lynd Ward. It not only displays many of Lynd's personal traits but highlights the attitude of a public unaware of the dynamic importance of his work. Lynd appears in the tape as an old man, but he still has the quick wit, verbal succinctness and mental capacity he was noted for by family and friends, so this interview has to be prior to the arduous years before he was disabled by Alzheimer's disease, which eventually took his life in June, 1985. Since he and the interviewer discuss the Abrams book on his wood engravings, *Storyteller Without Words*, published in December, 1974, the time of this interview is sometime after 1974.

In addition to being an archival tape of Lynd, including his own description of his work, this interview is a good example of early cablevision companies in the United States when airtime was filled in with long hours of public service announcements and interviews with local personalities. Depending on what part of the country you were living in, the subject of these local interviews could range from the re-election of the director of county sanitation to the editor of a church cookbook. The station owners served, in many cases, as the engineers and on-camera personalities who conducted the interviews, with little charisma or professionalism. Cable companies literally filled in airtime to keep their license agreements in those early years prior to network affiliation and public buy-in of cablevision.

The beginning of this interview shows a tall man wearing black pants and a striped oxford shirt. His clothes are disheveled and wrinkled, and his pale skin seems taut with signs of stress including fidgeting and quick, jerking head motions when he talks. His eyes bulge until he finally sits down on a chair beside another man, who is Lynd Ward.

Although an old man, Lynd is properly groomed, his long hair combed back off his forehead. Noticeably thick eyebrows shade his large dark eyes. He is dressed simply in a suit and tie which might have fit him a few years earlier but now hang just enough on his body to make the early signs of aged frailness noticeable. The camera remains static. The interviewer, from when we first see him rushing into camera view, is probably operating the camera himself and is probably the only staff person in the studio, which is why the camera's position during the interview remains static. This is confirmed when he sits down and glances at an on-air television set and notices that the camera eye is hugging far left. He stands up and adjusts the camera slightly so that both men are now centered on screen.

It is obvious from the very start of the interview that the interviewer has no idea who the man sitting beside him is or what the nature of his work is.

"Well," says the interviewer, who wipes sweat from his forehead on the sleeve of his shirt. "I am joined today by a local artist by the name of...." He pauses, and panic shows on his face for a moment before Lynd comes to the man's rescue and speaks his own name.

"... Lynd Ward," says Lynd in his low yet strong tone of voice that he was noted for. He pronounces his first name succinctly so it is not confused with the name Lynn.

The interviewer suddenly sees the cover of the book sitting on the table in front of him. "Oh yes, of course." He picks up the book. "Here you are." He raises the book in his

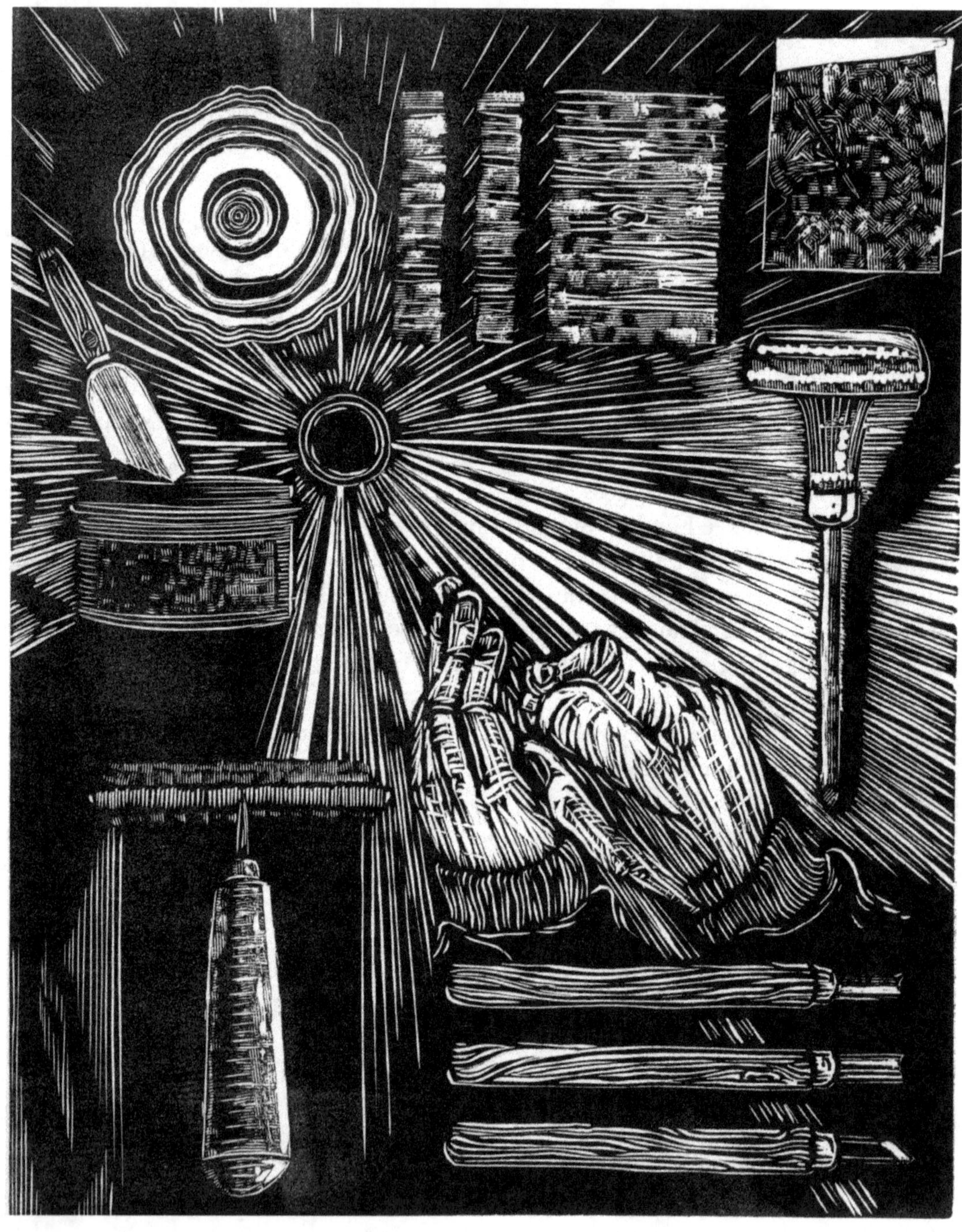

hand. He looks over at Lynd and makes a sly wink at the camera. The interviewer raises his other hand. "I mean, here you are." He laughs. Lynd blinks his eyes.

"Actually, *that* is where I am," says Lynd, pointing to the book that the interviewer sets back down on the table. Lynd never once during the interview looks at the camera, despite the prompts by the interviewer early in the interview. Lynd focuses specifically on the interviewer, who immediately becomes uncomfortable under Lynd's gaze, avoids Lynd's eyes, and speaks directly to the camera for most of the remaining interview.

"Well, let's see what kind of things you like to do," says the interviewer. He opens the large coffee table size book and flips through the pages. His reaction of surprise is expressed after flipping through only a couple pages. "Wow, look at some of these drawings." He holds the open pages of the book to the camera, but the engravings cannot be seen distinctly from this distance. It is obvious there is no one behind the camera, or they would have zoomed right in on the book. "There are some pretty heavy drawings here," says the interviewer, who draws out the word "heavy" as they did at that time in the '70s.

"They are not drawings," says Lynd.

"What do you mean?" asks the interviewer. "They look like drawings to me."

"They are called wood engravings."

"Wood carvings?"

"Engravings," corrects Lynd. "Do you know what an engraving is?"

The interviewer smiles awkwardly.

"Why don't you tell our audience what an engraving is," he says, swinging his arm from Lynd to the camera, trying to direct Lynd's attention to the camera. Lynd does not sway his attention from the interviewer as he explains in detail the process of wood engraving.

"The technique of the woodcut is simplicity itself. On the smooth surface of the block the artist proceeds to make a drawing in black ink, as loosely or as exact in detail as his temperament dictates. Every part of the wood that is not black must be cut away so that when a roller charged with ink passes over, only those parts that have been left at the original height will receive the ink. The cutting is done with a knife, the essential attributes of which are an exceedingly sharp edge and a form that will fit the hand easily.

"The old woodcutter sought to handle the knife so skillfully that every line laid down by the artist would come through without alteration. The modern artist works freely, taking advantage of accidental variation in the block, intensifying textures here, breaking down edges there, deriving stimulation from contact with the material.

"In wood engraving, the basic idea is the same: that is, to remove the parts of the block that are not to receive the ink from the roller. But the block is end-grain, sliced from the tree as you might slice bread from a loaf. The combination of end-grain block and graver permits of a finer line, more textural variation, and greater detail than is possible in the ordinary block cut with knife. In the hands of the modern artist, that fine line becomes the means of achieving a combination of subtlety and power unique in the graphic arts."

The interviewer cannot keep his eyes off Lynd's large hands. As Lynd describes the process of wood engraving, his hands respond almost in unison to the description. Like a trusted dog, his hands jump to the commands in Lynd's words. His fingers grasp the tools, push down or manipulate the block, his thumb brushes off the surface.

"Cutting a block is unlike anything else; it involves a struggle between an obdurate material on the one hand and a human will on the other. The wood is reluctant; the artist is determined, and inevitably something of the primitive clarity of the resulting antagonism is reflected in the forms that emerge as the cutting proceeds. Add to this the electrifying sweep of its color–brilliant white to richest black–the keen stimulation of its textural capacities, and you have the fundamental qualities for which the woodcut is valued by living artists."

The interviewer returns to flipping through the book after Lynd is finished speaking, and his hands are relaxed again on his lap.

"So these engravings," says the interviewer, putting emphasis on the word engravings, "are all carved in wood. I see some of them are brown instead of black and white. Is that from a different kind of wood?" It is hard to tell if the interviewer is joking or really is asking a question. He is probably just filling in airtime. If Lynd feels either way, he does not show any sign of irritation. Lynd was direct with everyone in his life and responded to others in kind, in this situation as well.

"No," says Lynd. "That is the color of the ink that I used to print the few prints that you mention. They are from my pictorial narrative, *Wild Pilgrimage*." Lynd spoke like he drew–every word, like every line he drew, was exact and especially chosen.

Lynd's tone is never critical, despite the insensitivity of the interviewer, who does not bother to hide his indiscretion when looking at his watch on numerous occasions. Lynd does not offer any information that is not asked, so the responsibility is placed, as it should be, on the interviewer, who finally shows a glimmer of relief after looking at his watch and happily bringing the interview to a close.

"Well, I want to wish you the best of luck with your engravings." The interviewer raises the Abrams book.

"Those are reprints," says Lynd.

"What?" asks the interviewer.

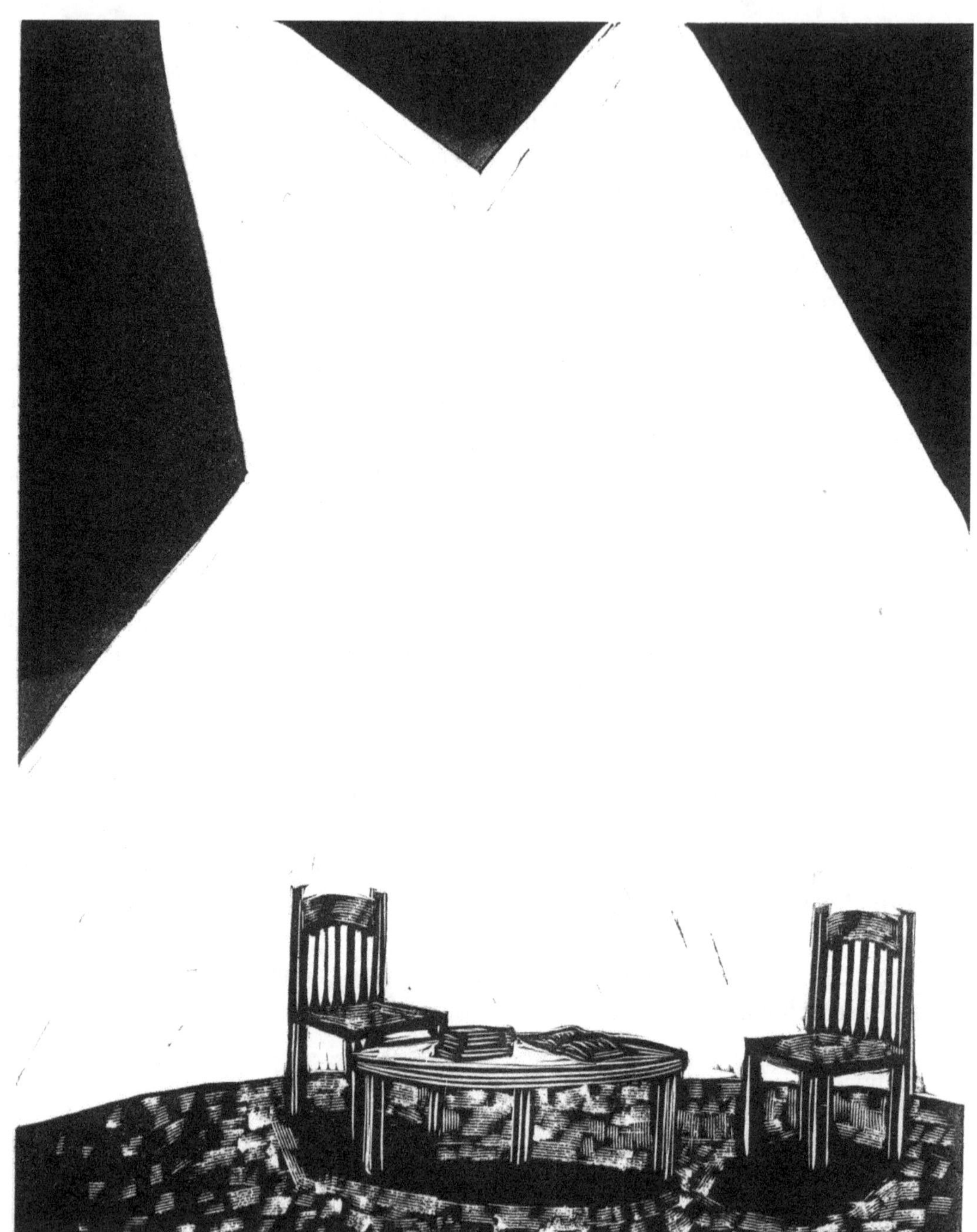

“The prints in the Abrams book are largely from books that were published as early as 1929.”

“Well,” interrupts the interviewer. “I’m sorry, but we don’t have anymore time to continue this....” He pauses, looking for the right word. Though “excruciating” would probably describe the interviewer’s experience on camera today, he chooses a canned phrase. “... interesting program with my guest, Mister Ward.” He fumbles in his pants pocket. “Join me next week when I will be sitting down with...” The interviewer flips a piece of paper over and shows a worried expression. “...another interesting personality from our cable neighborhood.” He smiles and stands up from his chair and then vanishes from the camera eye as he steps behind the camera.

There is one moment before the camera is turned off and the viewers are shown a static image of the cable affiliation. In this moment, Lynd Ward is shown sitting alone on his chair. His eyes are lowered to his large hands that skillfully engraved the wood blocks that established the foundation of pictorial narratives in the United States. He sits silently, patiently, alone with his thoughts.

Imagining

Harry Ward

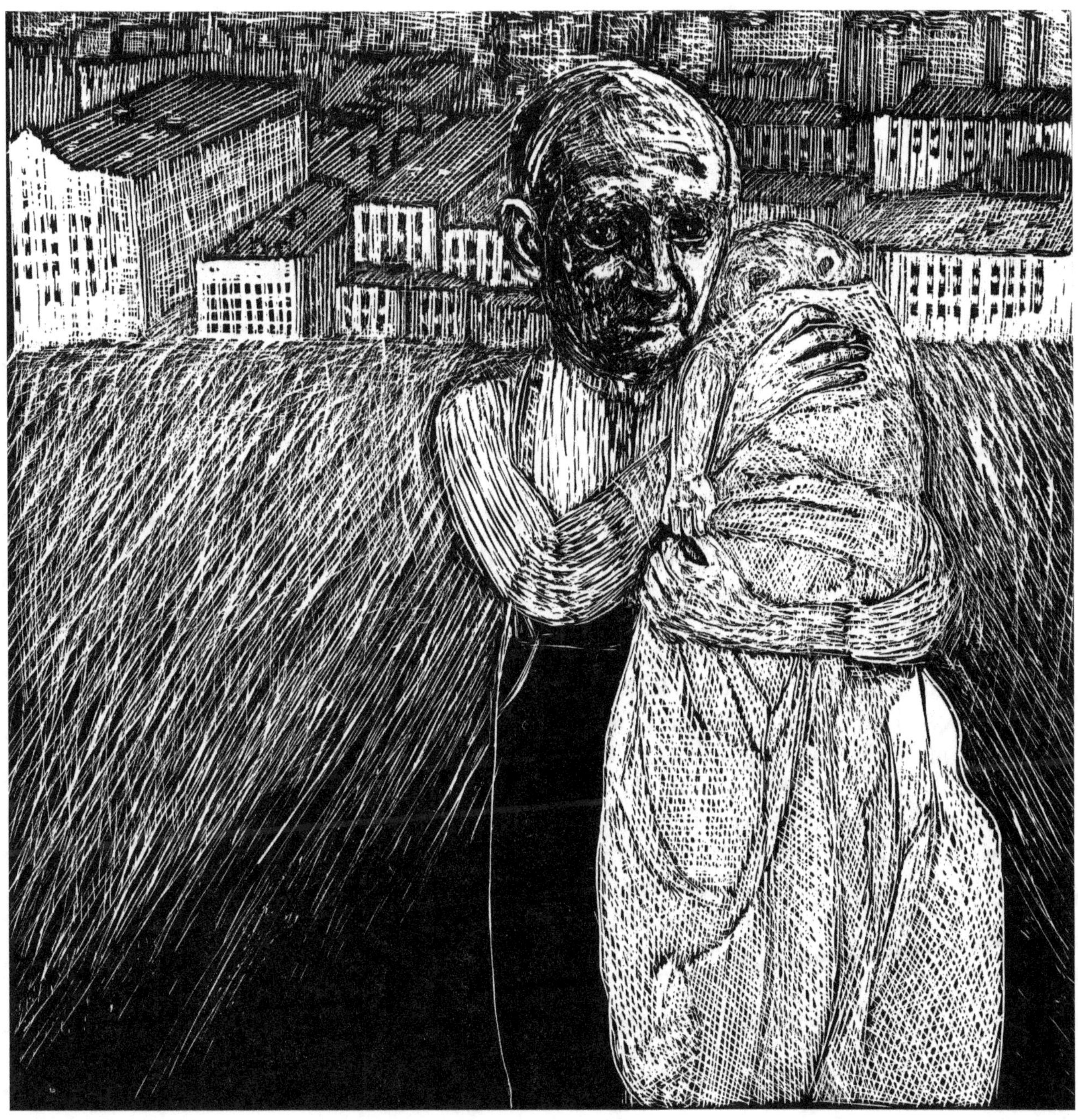

The infant Lynd begins squirming and whimpering, and Harry hears Daisy hushing the baby with soothing whispers. Harry is pulled back into his dream of the squalor in Chicago... with all the turmoil and pain rising like water, and he begins to struggle, fighting to stay alive, and trying to save people by pulling them to floating debris before they drown. Then he hears the cry of a baby and looks around and sees Lynd bobbing under the heavy hand of an industrialist who looks like a caricature by Art Young in the magazine, *The Masses*. As Harry tries to swim out to Lynd, someone pulls his arm, and there is a man with a thick mustache, speaking Russian, who is trying to use Harry as a buoy. Lynd cries again, and Harry jerks himself away from the panic stricken Russian. Harry swims madly toward Lynd, who gurgles water as he sinks under the industrialist who has made a raft of babies like Lynd to keep himself afloat. Harry spurs like a fish out of water and knocks the industrialist off the raft of babies. Their heads bounce to the surface, gasping for air. Harry reaches for Lynd, but he is no longer breathing, and Harry screams, holding his child in his hands before he hears Daisy's voice holler out to him.

"Harry!" Daisy shakes Harry's shoulder, and he ascends out of his nightmare to the bed where he slowly senses where he is and hears the crying Lynd. "Are you alright?"

"Yes, yes," says Harry, slowly gaining consciousness.

"You were having a nightmare," says Daisy, "and I thought I better wake you before you punch me in the eye. You were swinging your arms and hollering." Lynd suddenly begins crying in earnest.

Harry sits up and reaches for a match on the night table. He strikes a match and lights an oil lamp that slowly brightens the rustic room. Harry looks down at Lynd and a smile comes to his face.

"I thought that we had lost you," says Harry, reaching for Lynd and raising him off the bed. He holds him for a moment and then places him back on the bed before putting on his pants and boots.

"Where are you going?" asks Daisy, still whispering, not to wake Gordon in a small single bed beside their bed.

"I'm taking Lynd for a moonlight stroll."

"But it is dark out."

"There's the moonlight, Daisy. God's streetlight for the somnambulists."

Daisy knew not to argue with Harry when his mind was made up.

"You go back to bed," said Harry. "I'm taking Lynd outside with me."

There is a light in the woods that is well known to anyone familiar with the woods. It

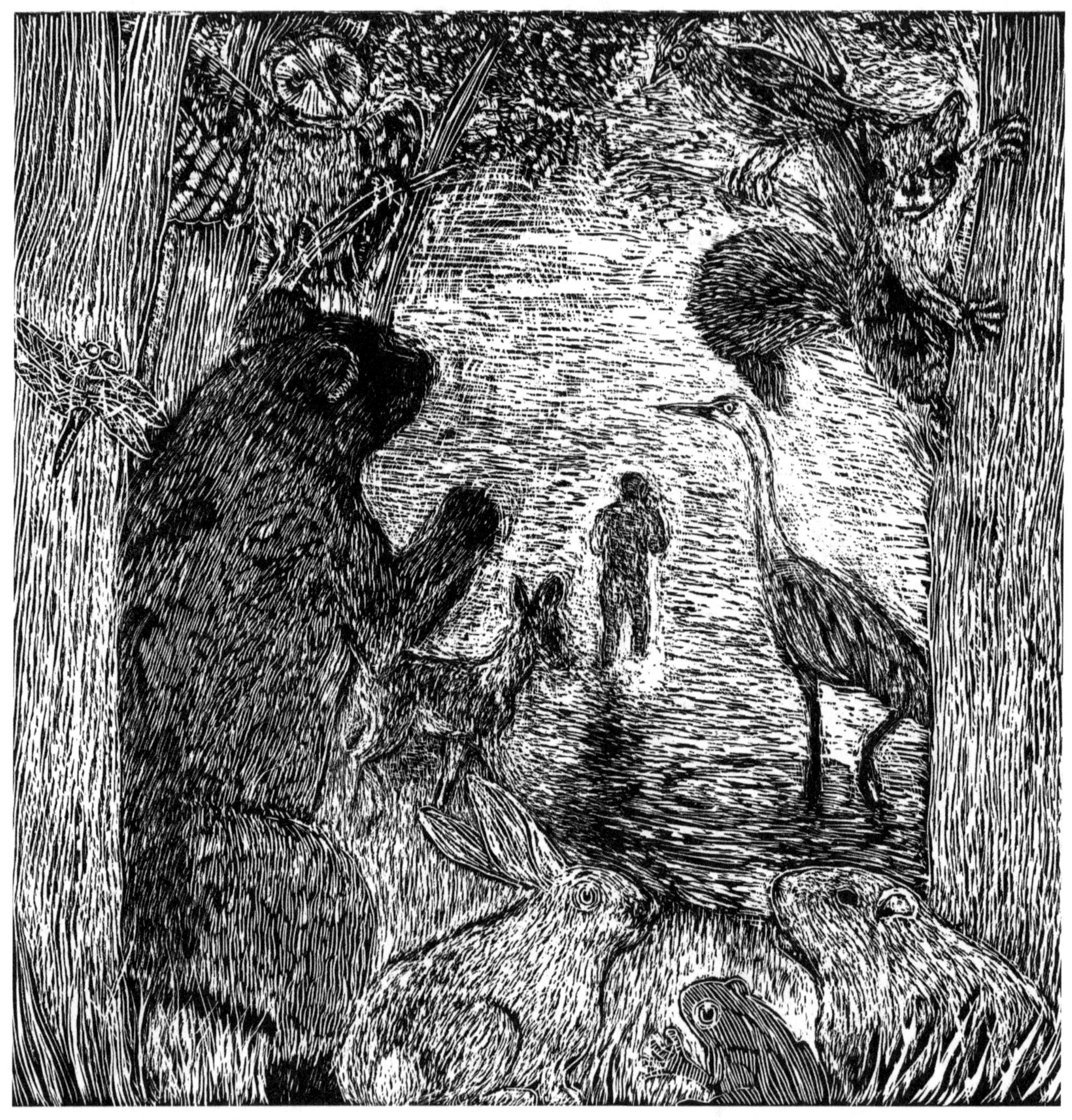

is a combination of our eyes adjusting to the darkness and the clearness of the sky, the glow from the stars and, if there is a moon present, brightness that is unmatched in any urban or suburban setting. You have to get out into the woods, far removed from any artificial light to experience the feeling of starlight and moonlight. If you have not experienced this yet in your life, you are missing out on an essential part of nature.

When Harry stepped outside, his feet already knew the dips on the trail to the water's edge. The bugs were out, but Harry covered Lynd's body with a light blanket with a small opening to breathe. Harry knew that the mosquitoes did not sleep, but they did not seem as prevalent as they had earlier in the evening. Perhaps they also knew the importance of this rite, Harry thought innocently.

It was a moment when Harry felt overwhelmed by the presence of God. Here was nature in all her glory. The calm still waters of Lonely Lake and the chirping of bugs and small animals filled the night air–a cacophony of sounds that Lynd's whimpering and Harry's breathing joined. This was an easy place to find God, and here in this forest Harry would find the grace from nature to rejuvenate his body and spirit so that he could re-enter the other world that man was making in the cities.

Harry had first thought that perhaps he would baptize young Lynd on the shore of Lonely Lake, but he suddenly felt so much a part of the natural world around him that he found himself slowly stepping out of his shoes and clothes. Naked, he lifted Lynd out of the blanket and slipped him out of his diaper. Harry stepped over the rocks near the boat ramp and waded out into the cool water. The darkness of the water and the eerie quietness were soothing, and he felt as though the hand of God was holding him as he now held Lynd. Harry waded out to his chest and cradled Lynd close to his face. Lynd had stopped whimpering, and his eyes blinked and stared directly into Harry's eyes before he noticed the moon and the stars. Here was a cup of sky that Lynd would always return to drink from and find sustenance. Lynd reached out and lifted himself on Harry's stare, which held him up to catch the stars in his infant's hand. His hands were extremely active, though he was silent. Harry

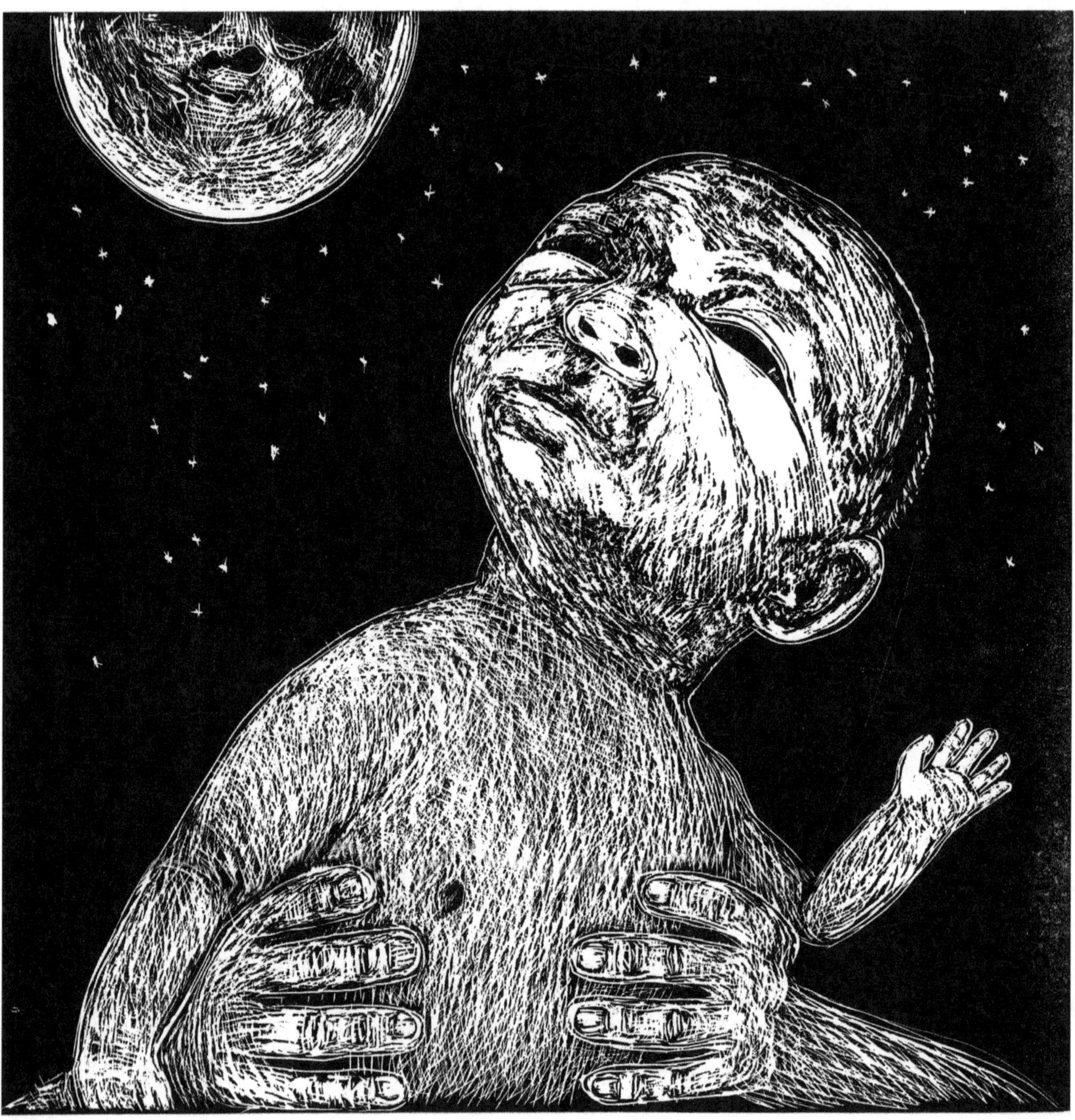

watched as Lynd twirled his fingers around as though he was drawing with his fingers a line between each star in the galaxy. Harry watched as his son's attention was directed to the heavens and wondered what was going on inside Lynd's head.

"Well, you are already a dreamer," said Harry, "with your head up in the stars."

"This will cure you of any ailment," said Harry. At that moment, Harry felt the minnows nimble on his chest, perhaps on a scab or a cut. "Wait until I finish my work here," said Harry, "and then you can chew on my ashes." Harry held Lynd's naked body close to his as he waded out of the water, stepping carefully on the bank where he set Lynd down inside his blanket before he dressed and went back to the cabin.

At night when Lynd would cry and in the afternoon when Lynd would get aggravated and tired before his nap, Harry would take him down to the lake, which seemed to comfort him with the slow rhythm and motion of the water in unison with Harry's breathing. Throughout the summer months Lynd and Harry's bond grew.

Back in Chicago, neighbors claimed Harry had made a miraculous recovery, but he dismissed their claims because he knew the healing power of nature. It had saved his life, and there was no reason why his son would not have benefited as well. This was the beginning of a bond that would link Lynd to Harry and Lonely Lake for the rest of his life.

Imagining

Lonely Lake

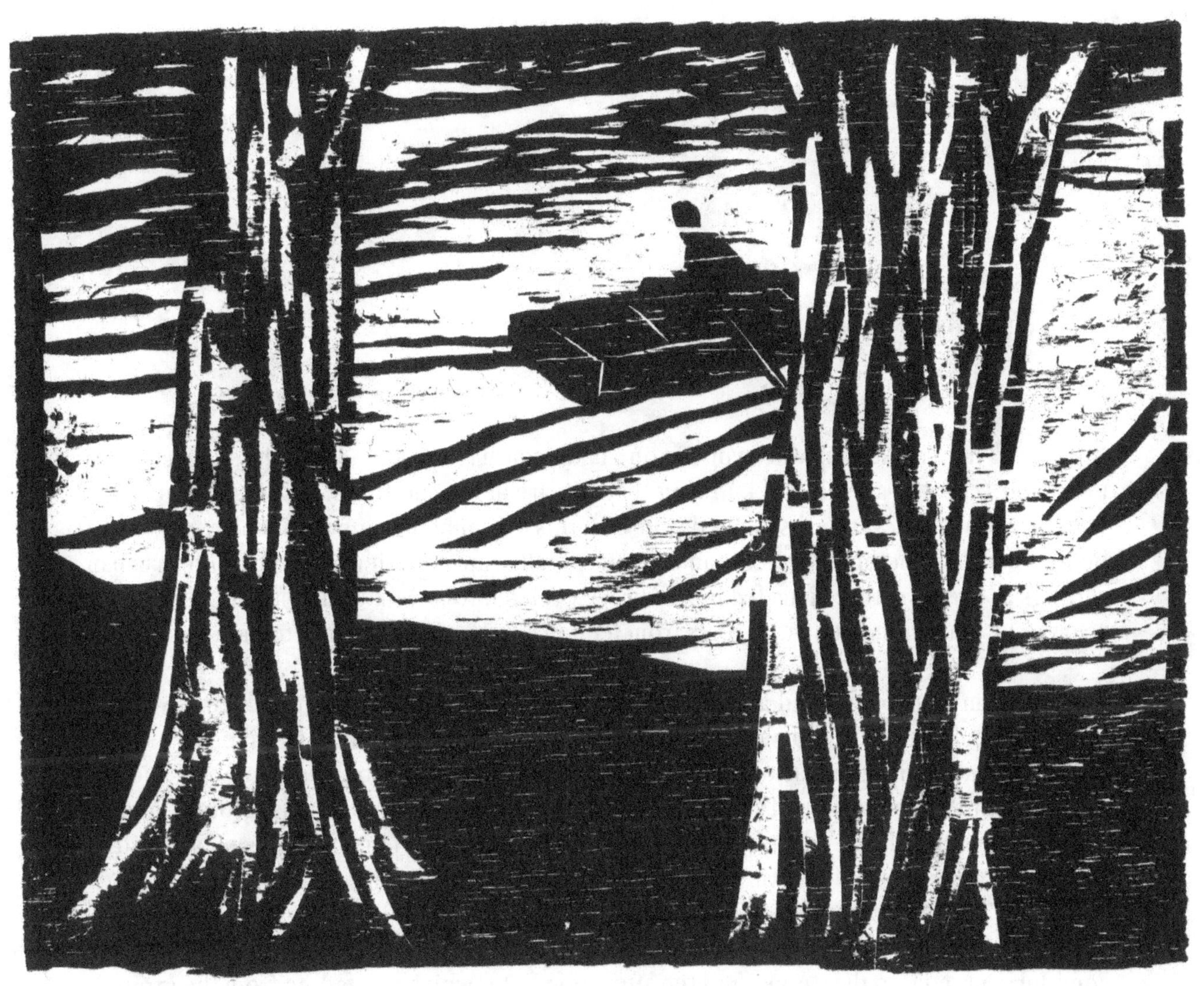

There is a feeling when you are on a lake or on a river alone, when the silence comes upon you. There is a feeling of knowing that you are alone and that if some accident befell you, that you may never be discovered. But with this fear of being alone also comes a grasp of being a part of something greater than oneself, which is not experienced as strongly in urban settings as it is in nature. This feeling is directly related to our natural instincts, though we seem to be getting further and further from feeling anything like kinship to nature.

From birth, Lynd had a direct connection to nature and certainly to Lonely Lake. He thought about this feeling as he rowed a boat down the river alone. He liked to hug the shoreline and catch a glimpse of a deer or a fox, and look down into the green water and see twenty or thirty feet deep, and sometimes see a large bass. This was his playground, and he loved it as much as he loved anyone in his life, including May, whom he had been married to for only a couple years. This was her second summer visit to the lake.

Lynd heard a noise in the woods and held his oars still in the water so as not to make a sound. He gazed into the woods, and the afternoon light, which was fading from the ground,

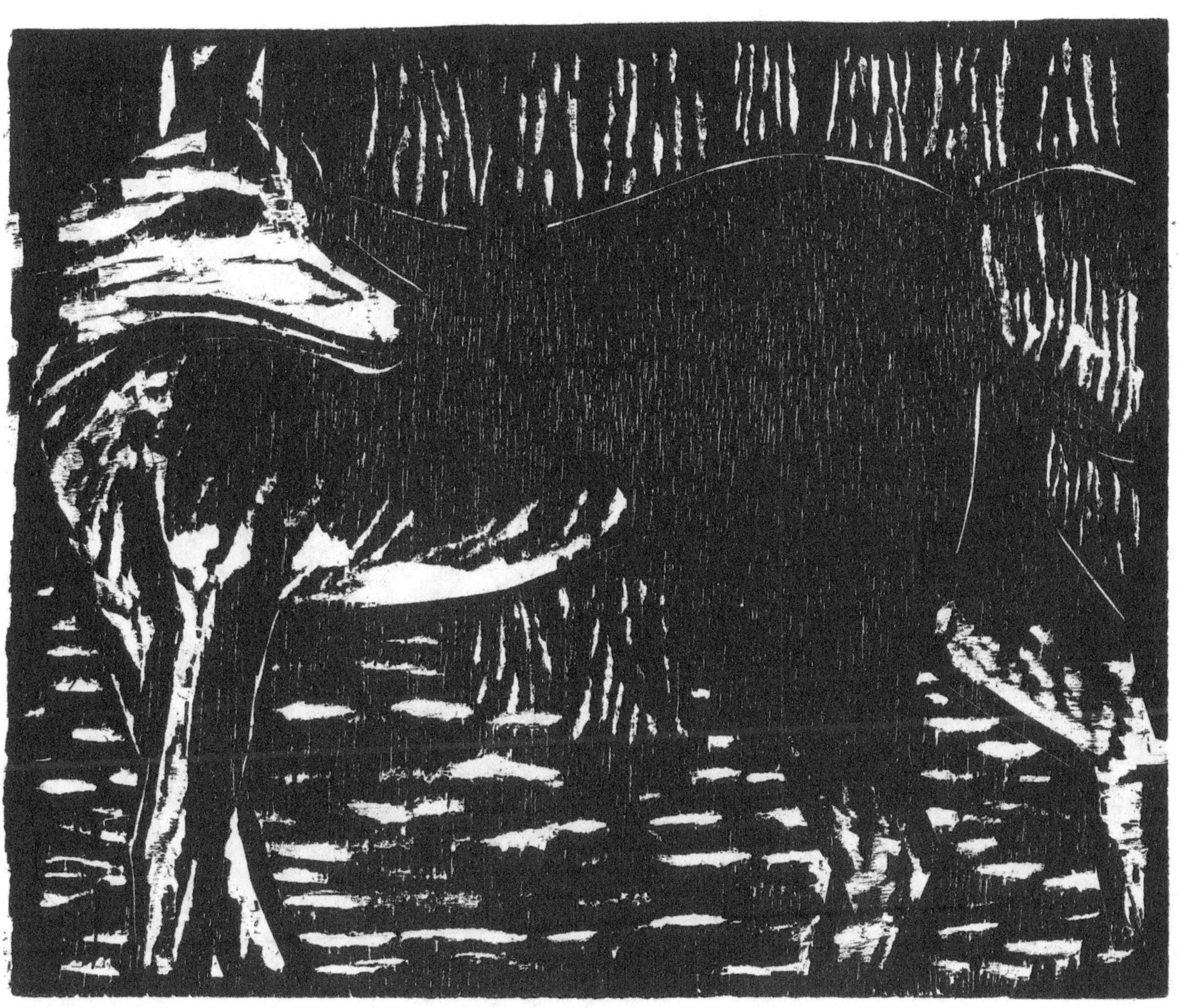

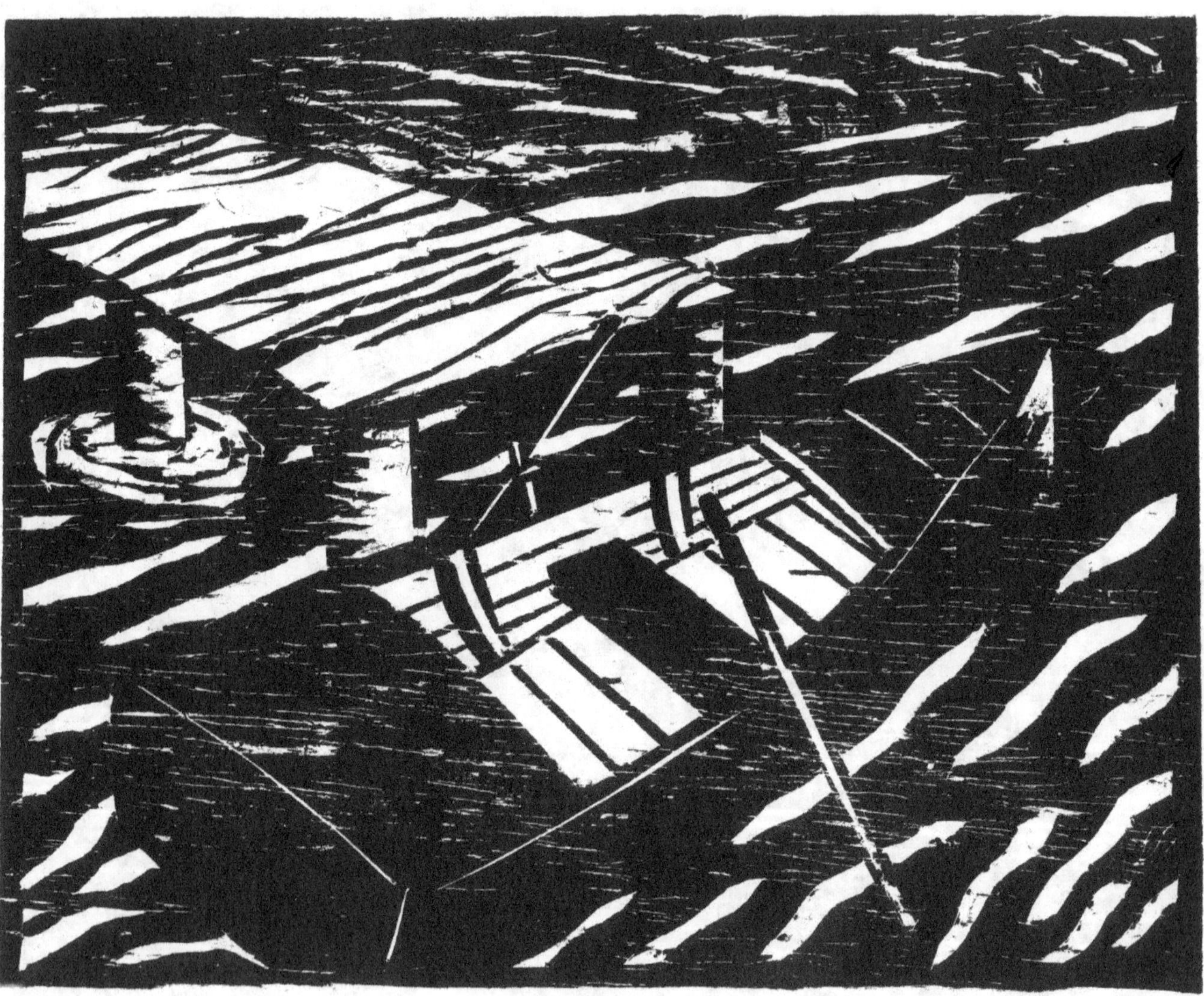

created tunnels of darkness where shapes could hide. He remained still because he knew he had heard something large. Maybe a moose or even a bear. He gazed into the woods for the longest time but could not see anything. Whatever was in the woods was probably watching him as well and maybe thought it would be nice to return to his lair and report that he had seen a human on the lake. Lynd smiled at the thought. And then something moved. It was larger than any bear he had ever seen, but still remained black and hidden in the shadows, its movement not out of fear of being seen.

Lynd pulled on his oars and moved slowly back away from the shore. There was a fear in his heart that something walked in his woods that he could not name. He guessed what this black figure represented, then suddenly became alarmed. His rowboat began to rock, and he turned his attention to the lake that was getting choppy. A storm was approaching. He dug his feet into the rib of the boat and began to row quickly back across the lake to the cabin. As the storm waters rose, the choppy waves gathered momentum and slapped across the side of his boat. He would let his boat fall within the dip of a wave and glide with the wave for a few yards before rowing over it and catching another dip. This was the only way he was able to gain any distance across the lake, and after an exhausting trial that took hours, Lynd came up to the boat pier.

He did not mention the dark shadow in the woods to anyone, but he would recall it many times in his future and would personify it in many of his books.

Imagining

May McNeer

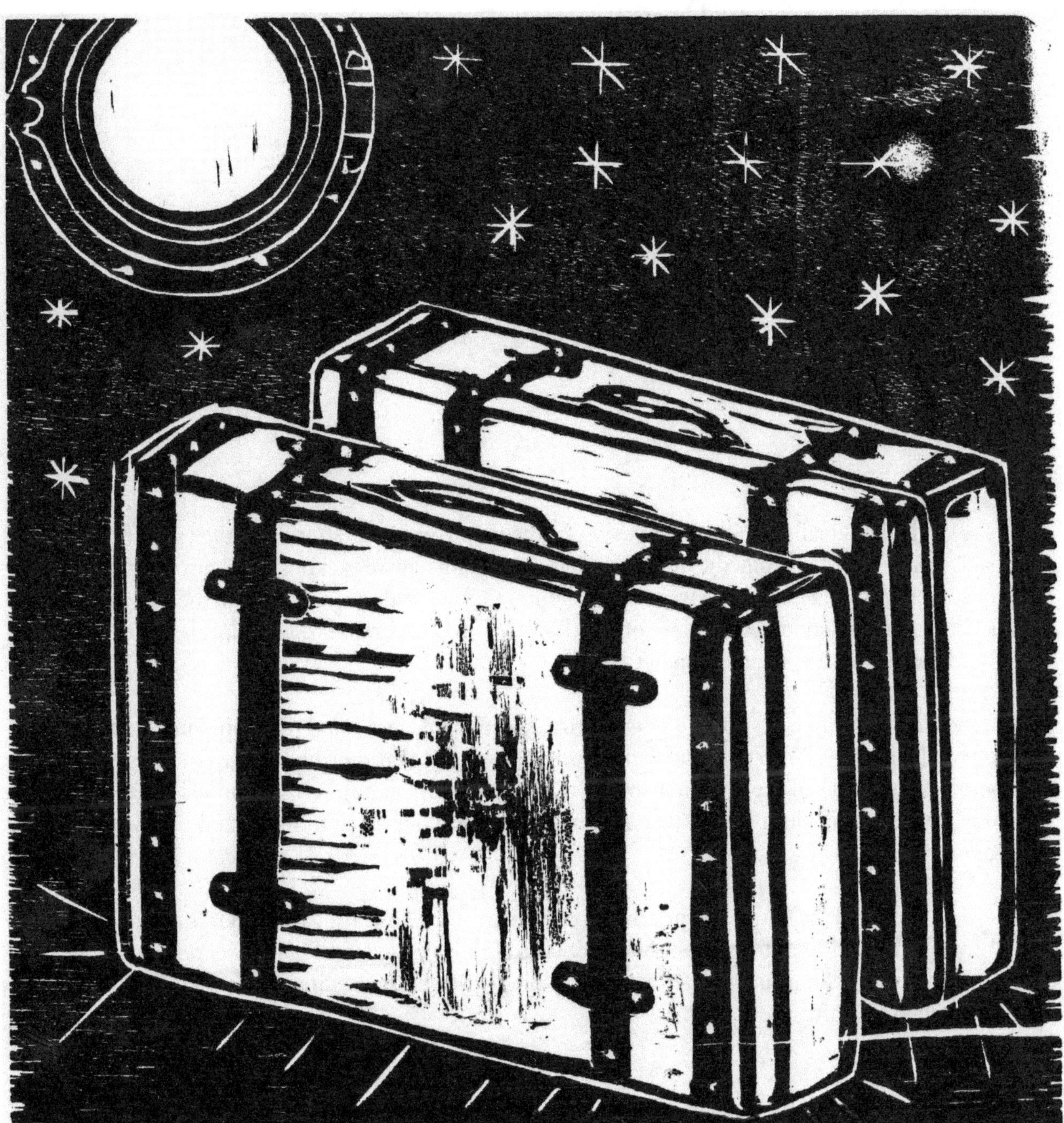

They finally reached their cabin in the ship *Carmania* after what they would look back on as a slapstick comedy, but at the time, was a most nerve racking set of circumstances for both Lynd and May. In a matter of a few hours, they were alone in a room on their wedding night, and the sudden nervousness of the day paled in comparison to the apprehension that they both felt at the present moment.

Their cabin was small with two chairs, a small table and a bed that could not be overlooked by the newly married bride and groom. It was not that they had never been together before, but those had been moments when they kissed, with mouths closed, or he had cradled May's head on his chest in dark movie theaters, or held her close to him when they walked together at night.

They had the entire journey over to Germany to get to know each other "in that way." Why was it so difficult to say it. Sex. Lynd wanted to just say it, and maybe its power would vanish from the room and release its grip on him. Lynd set their suitcases down on the bed. He opened his suitcase.

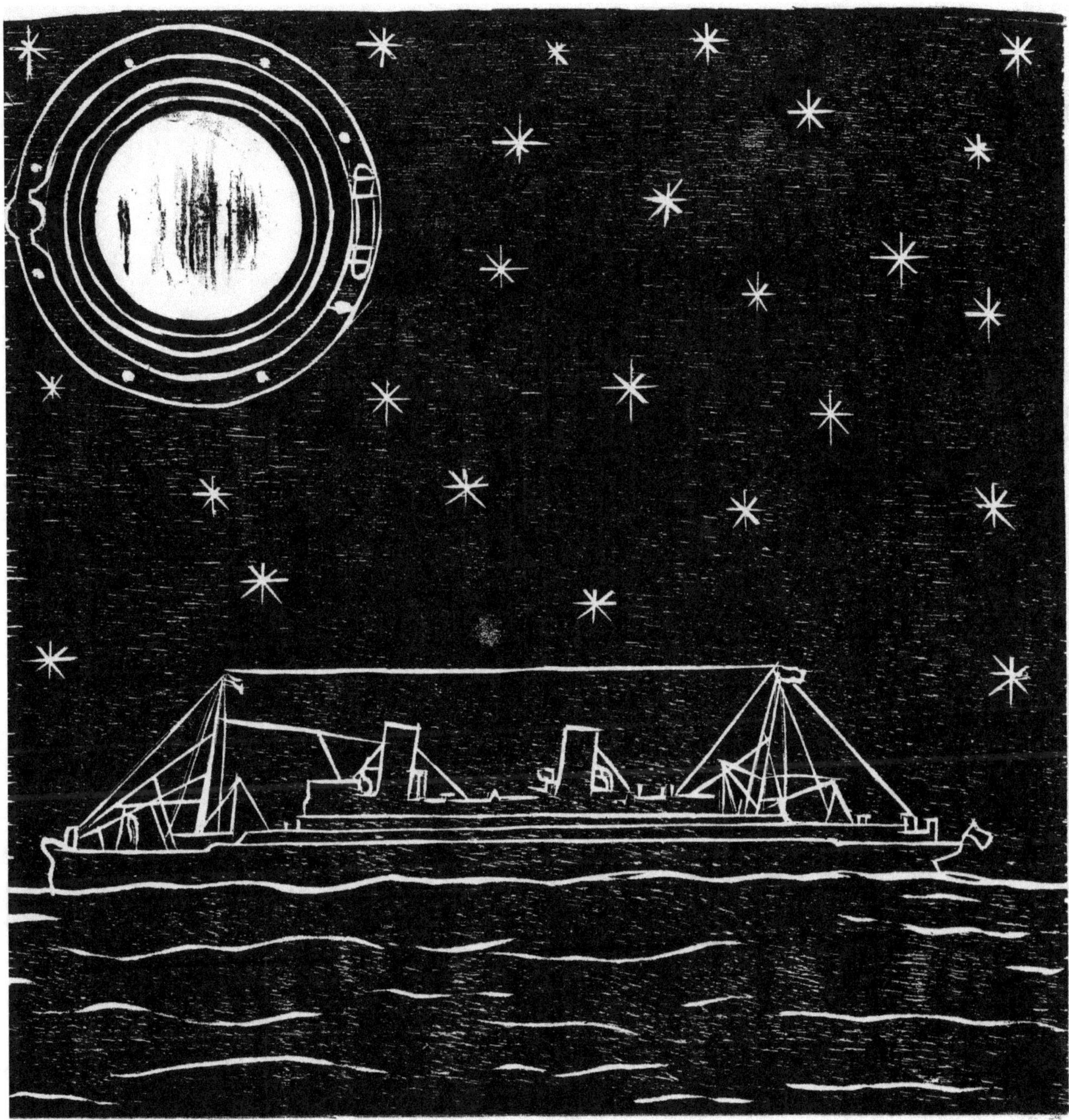

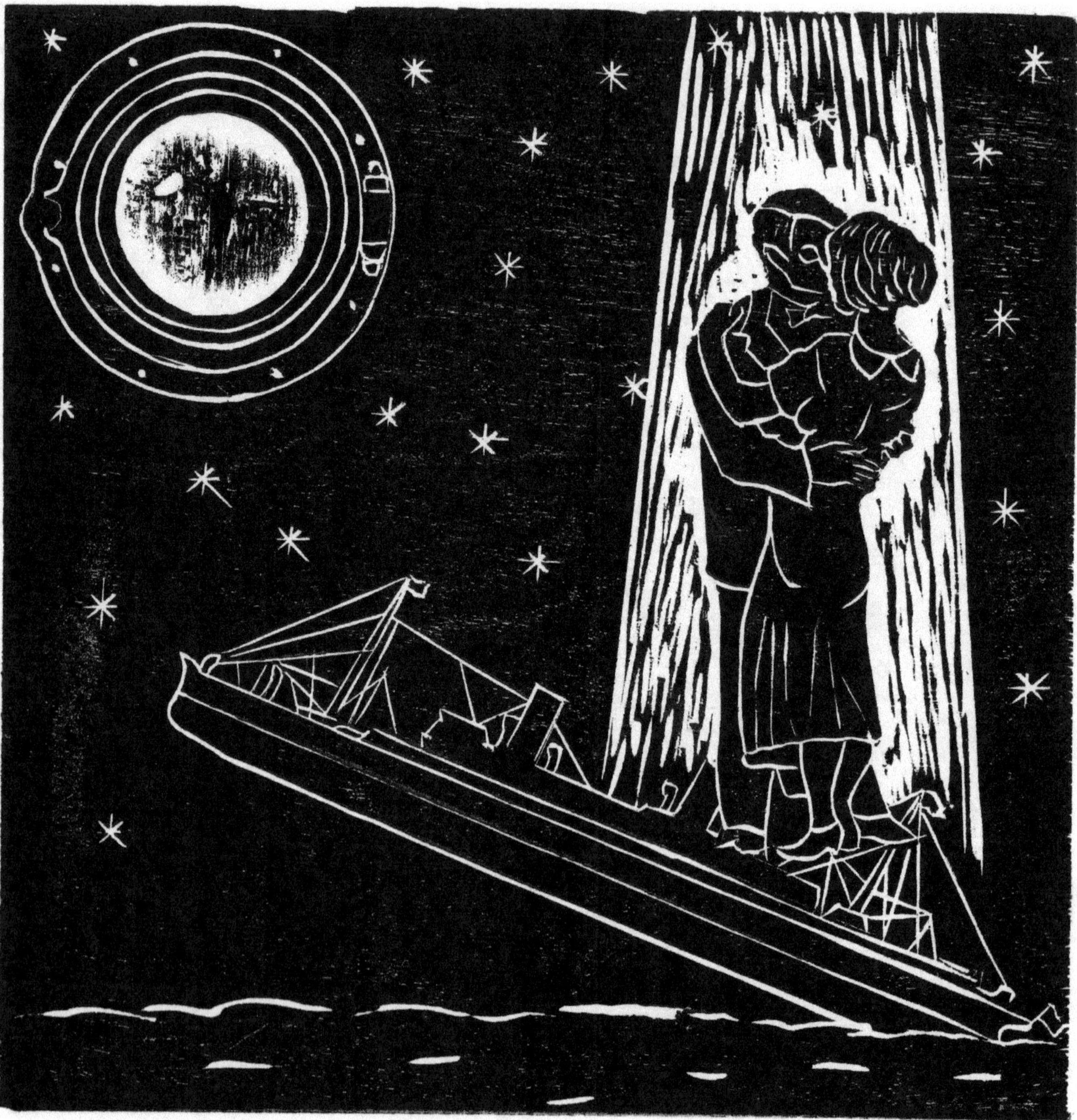

"Let me do that," said May. She also could not think straight and was as frightened of their wedding night as Lynd was, though neither spoke a word of it. May just wanted to keep busy and fill in the time before they went to bed. There wasn't any rule that said that they had to "do it" tonight. Was there?

May opened one of four drawers in the dresser and began putting Lynd's clothes away. Lynd looked over at May's suitcase. Both suitcases were made of leather, though May's had certainly seen more wear. Lynd stepped around May and opened her suitcase.

"What are you doing?" asked May, startled.

"You get to look at mine," Lynd said, glancing down at his suitcase. "I can't let you have all the fun." He smiled.

That seemed to break the nervousness they both felt. May smiled back and then placed her hands on the side of Lynd's face. Blue eyes met blue eyes as the blaring of the *Carmania's* loud whistle rose in their room, and the ship moved away from the harbor. A tear filled May's eyes and fell down her cheek. Lynd had placed his hands on May's hips, and when he saw the tear fall down her cheek, he moved close to her face and kissed the tear on her cheek and then over to her lips which she opened slightly for him.

Imagining

Woodcut Novels

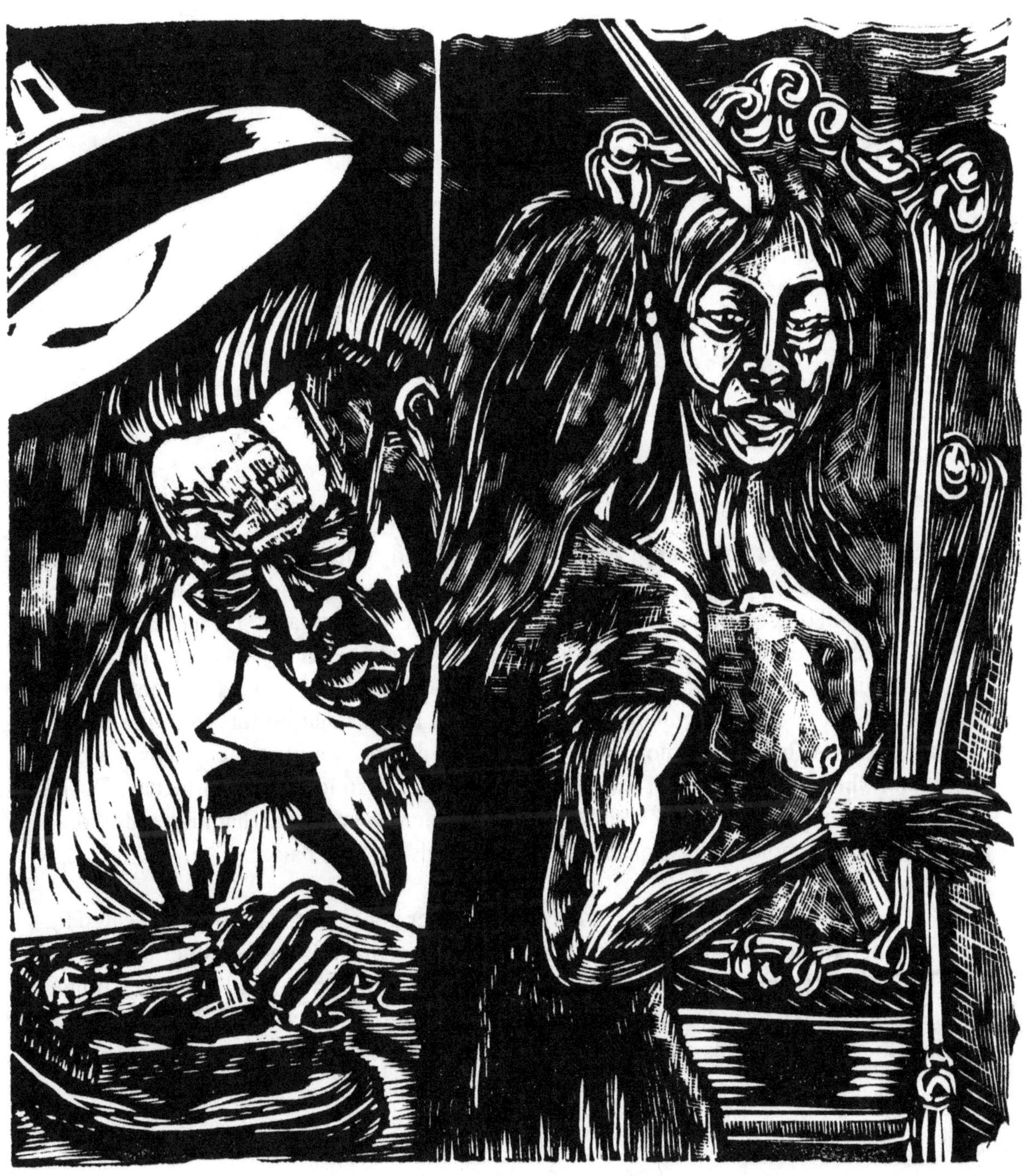

After dinner, Lynd went back to his studio and continued working on the blocks for his woodcut novel, *Vertigo*. After working for a few minutes, Lynd began to experience a loss of place and time. That was the only way he could describe it later. He had experienced a few of these episodes in the past, and they always occurred when he was engraving a block for a woodcut novel and, later, when he was working on his larger prints. This episode came just like the last one he remembered, with the initial feeling that he was stepping outside his own body. At first he was not aware of it. He leaned back and stretched his neck and shoulders, which were sore from leaning over his work for so long during the day. During the moment that he stretched back his head and shoulders, he realized that his hands did not pause, and he saw more of his own shoulders and finally his own back.

Lynd stood up and looked over his own shoulder of his seated figure. His seated figure continued to move his block of wood in one hand on a turntable as his other hand held a graver and sliced through the surface of the hard maple as though it was butter. His fingers worked quickly, like a spider spinning a web. There was an animated drama being played out right in front of his eyes on the block of wood. The objects and characters in the design

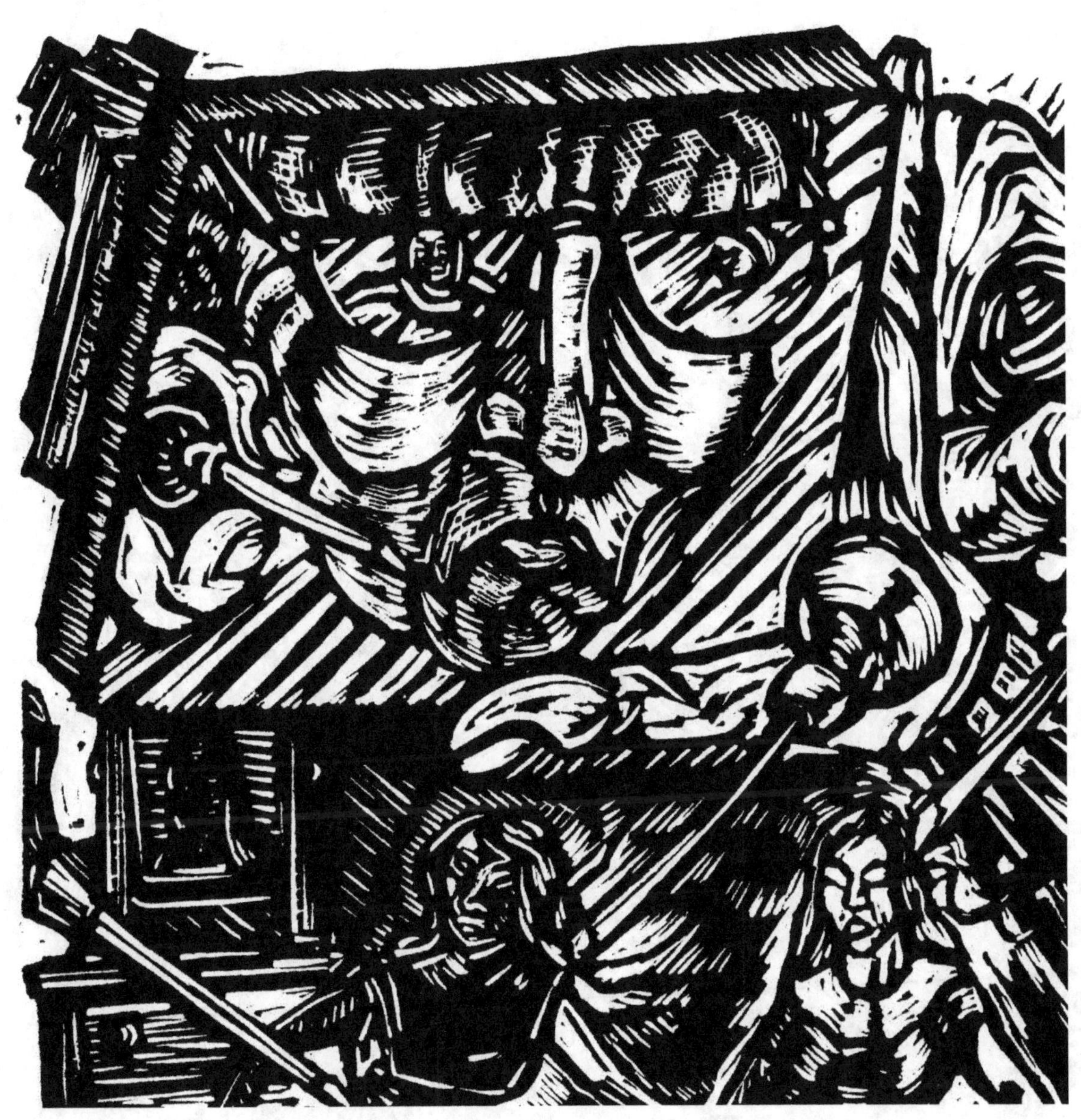

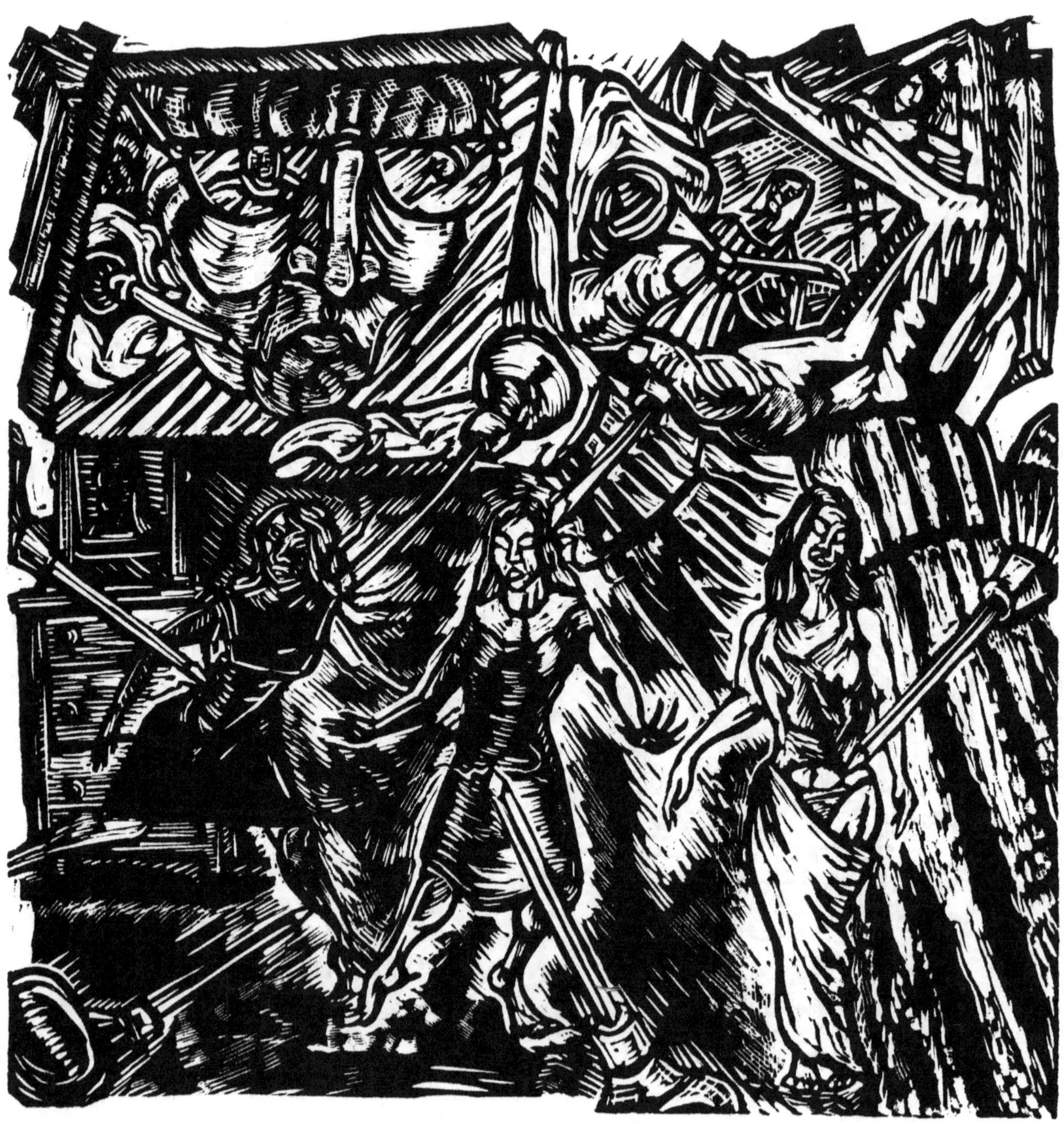

on the block were jumping around trying to avoid his graver and spit sticker that he switched from the table to his hand, swiftly like a doctor in surgery. The ghost of Lynd was happily watching as the point of his tools pinned down a dresser that he quickly cut out in the wood using a series of scorpers, chisels, and tint tools, in addition to his graver and spit sticker. In this scene, there was a woman, fully dressed, who immediately tried to hide behind the dresser to escape capture from his tools. However, he was able to nudge her out from behind the dresser with his graver and placed her standing in front of the dresser. He cut a mirror over the dresser for her to gaze in, and like King Kong holding Fay Wray in his hands, Lynd slowly cut the clothes off her figure. She lifted her arms high into the air, and he slowly cut her naked body into the surface of the wood.

In the next moment, the ghost of Lynd slipped from watching over his own shoulder. He slipped back into his own frame and flowed down to his fingertips. He dripped out into the block and then reassembled himself into a smaller figure of himself. He stood in front of the naked woman. At first she covered her breasts in surprise and then looked more closely at him standing in front of her. She glanced up from the block to the giant Lynd who had suddenly stopped working and only stared down at them like a statue.

"I'm sorry," she said. "I didn't know who you were at first."

"I hope I didn't frighten you," said Lynd.

"Frighten me?" she asked with a grin. She lowered her arms. He gazed at her naked figure. She stepped close to him and began to unbutton his shirt.

"Do you think we should be doing this?" asked Lynd.

"You're the only one watching," she said.

Lynd glanced up at the giant Lynd looking down at them and smiled.

When he awakened from his trance, his smaller self did not appear anywhere on the block. He felt light headed for a moment or two and then was suddenly surprised to hear the woman on the block whisper his name.

"Lynd... Lynd... are you coming to bed?"

Lynd dropped the tools in his hands before raising his head to the sound of his name being called louder.

"Lynd."

He looked up from the block on his table and turned around to face May in the doorway.

"It's three o'clock in the morning," May said. "Are you coming to bed?"

"Yes," he said. "I'll be right there." He picked up a multiple tint tool and glided it through the wood above the woman's head, bringing in a dazzling light over her body.

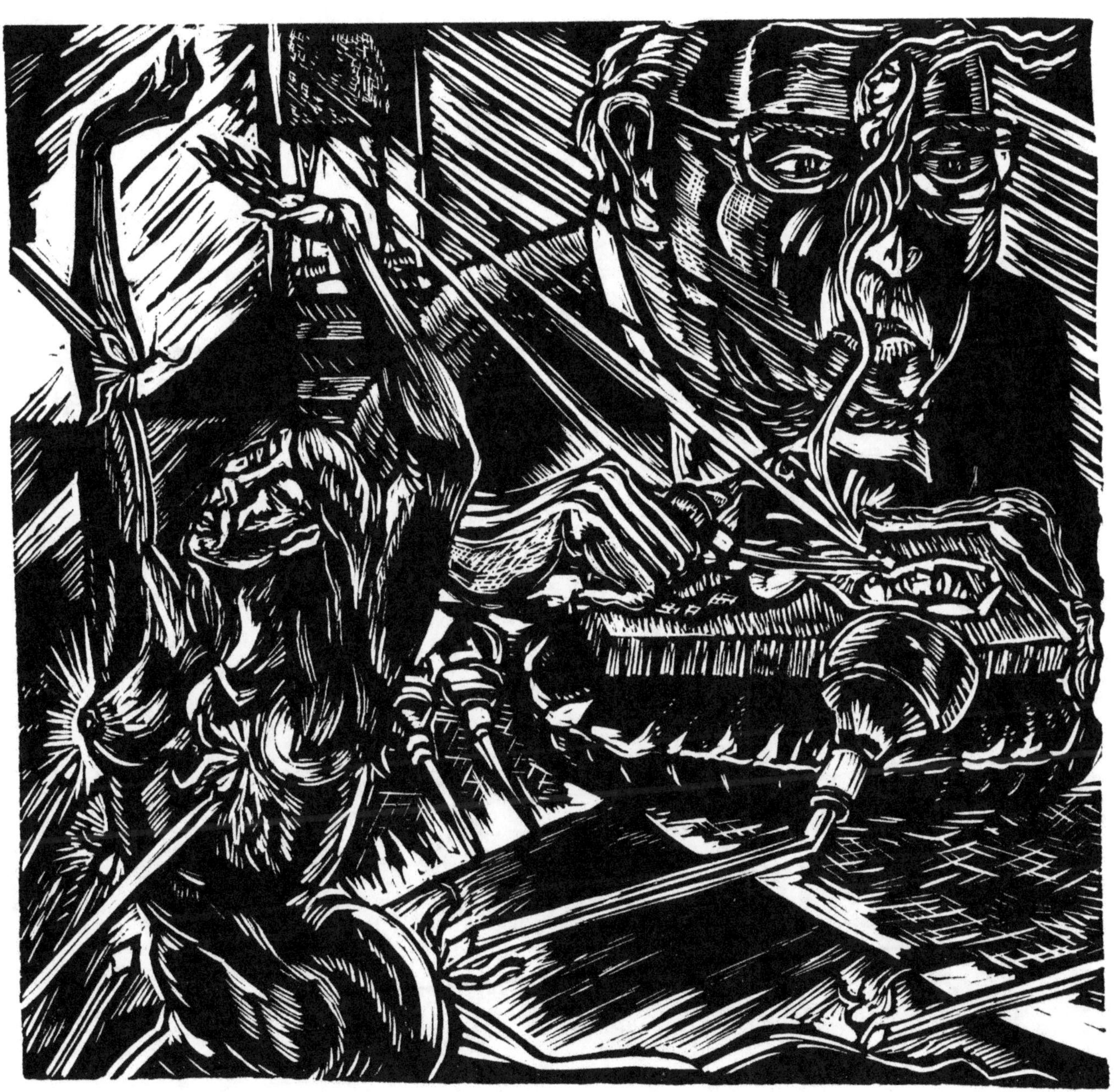

Imagining

Children's Books

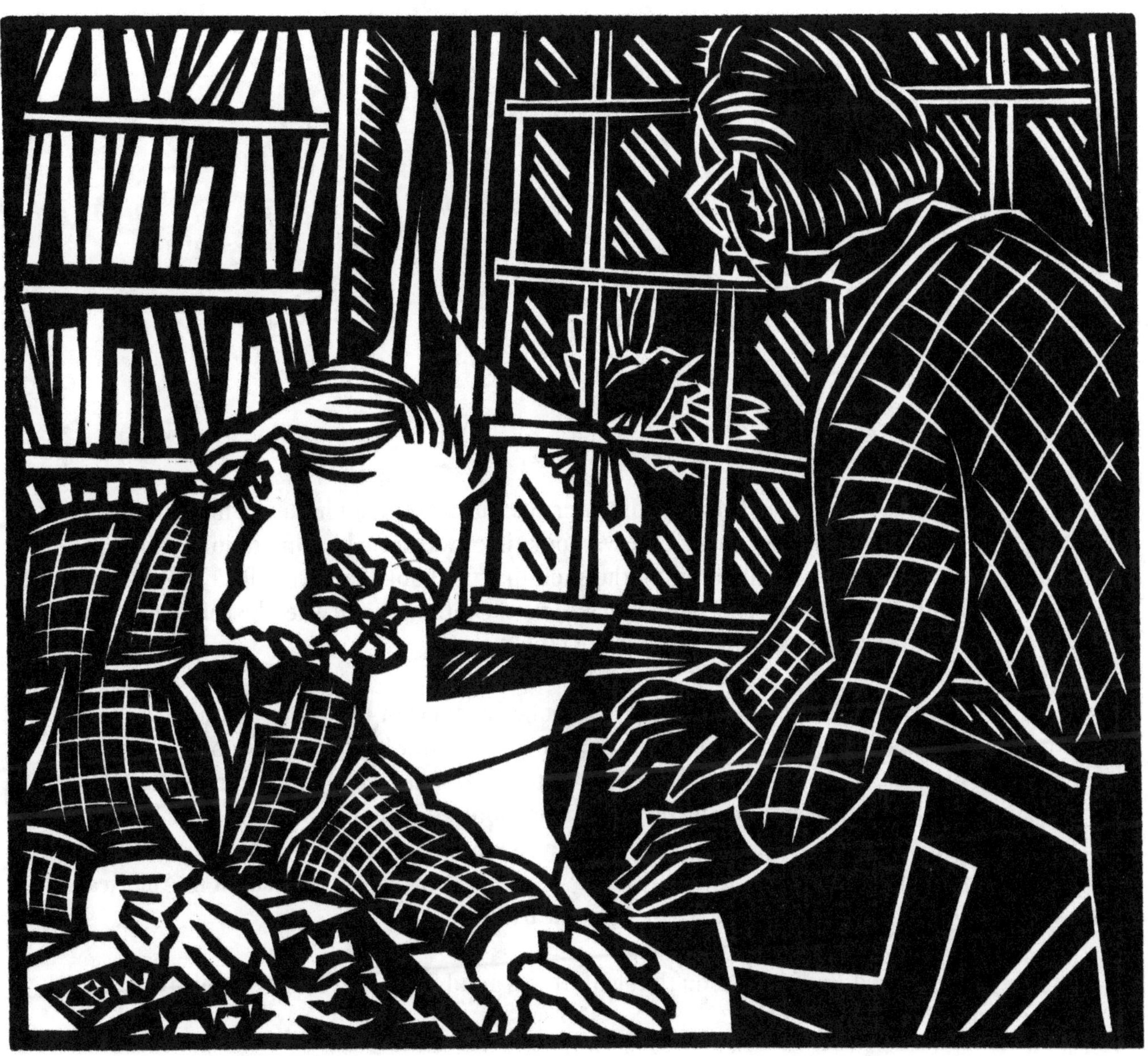

Lynd arrived home from Bendix later than usual, and after eating his dinner, he went into his studio. His work during the war took time away from his illustrations. His early success seemed to have been placed on the shelf like the books in his studio. Was his life now just building gyroscopes for Bendix? This was the difficult time when he had to find the courage to move his tired body to his drawing table.

Tonight he went to his bookshelf and looked at some of the books that he had illustrated–more than 50, not including his woodcut novels. How he loved the woodcut novels. He took one down from the shelf. It happened to be *Vertigo*, which had been his last. He remembered how much work was involved with that book and how cutting the blocks became as much of his daily life as breathing–perhaps even more important. *Vertigo* was more than an account of the Depression. It was Lynd's own political and spiritual account of America, and one that he would always hold close to his heart.

Lynd placed *Vertigo* back on the shelf. It was good for him to draw from his past. He sat down at his drawing table.

E DRAGONS
TO HEAVEN
IL'S CAVE
SPARROW
IEGFRIED
NFOREST
TOP TIM
NG SHOPS
THE BEAR
NG DEER
ACKNOSE
BANTAM
IFMAID
MAD MAN'S DRUM
WILD PILGRIMAGE
VERTIGO
GODS MAN
PRELUDE TO A MILLION YEARS
WITHOUT
STORY
SONG
KBW
SIR B
TOP
THE
LIT
LOLA
CH

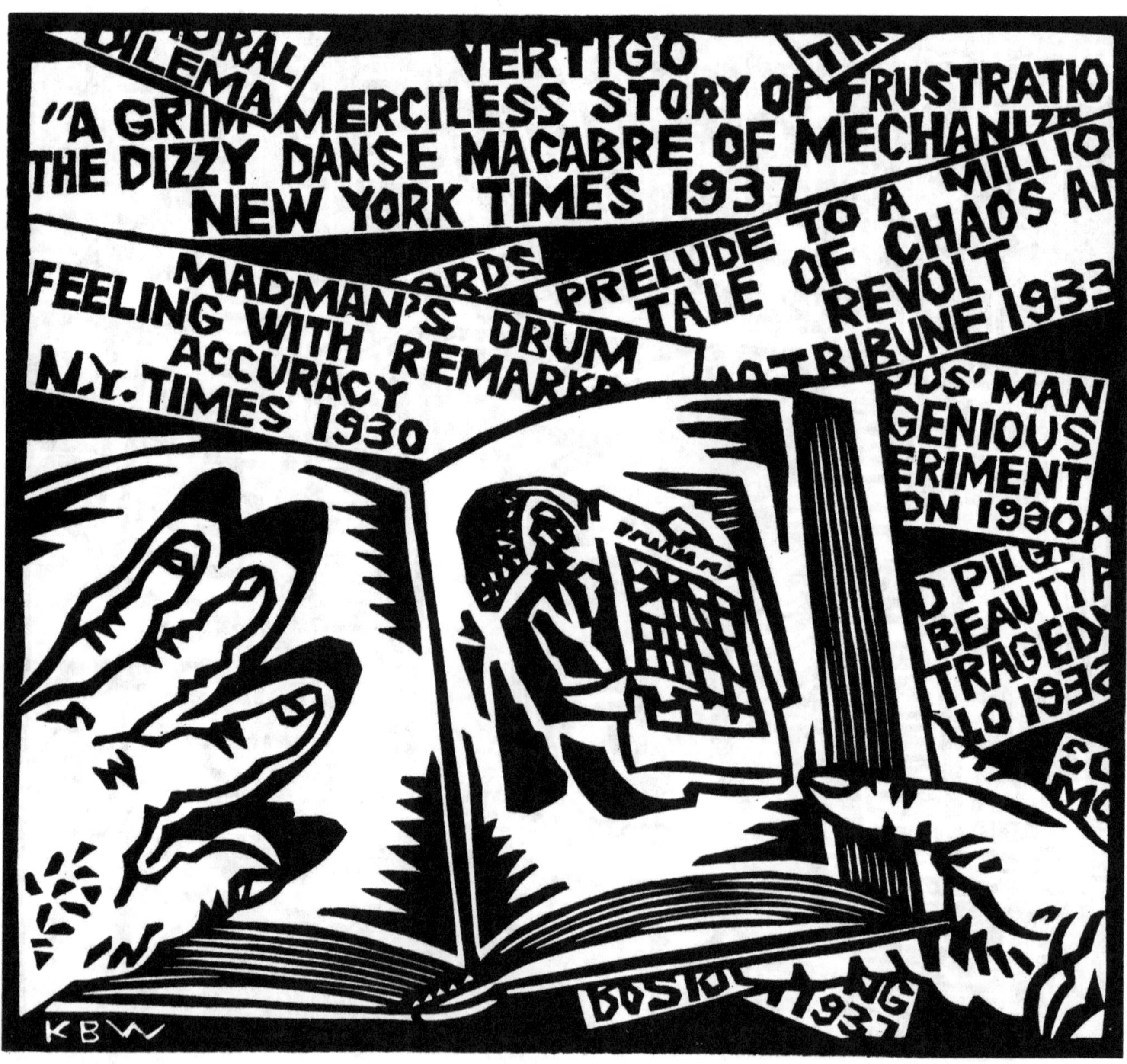

DILEMA
VERTIGO
"A GRIM MERCILESS STORY OF FRUSTRATIO
THE DIZZY DANSE MACABRE OF MECHANIZ
NEW YORK TIMES 1937
PRELUDE TO A MILLIO
TALE OF CHAOS A
REVOLT
TRIBUNE 1933
ORDS
MADMAN'S DRUM
FEELING WITH REMARKA
ACCURACY
N.Y. TIMES 1930
DS' MAN
GENIOUS
ERIMENT
ON 1930
D PILG
BEAUTY
TRAGEDY
LO 1930
1937
KBW

He found that once he was seated at this table and began drawing on the project at hand, then his doubts and misgivings dissolved. After a few moments the work took hold of his senses, and he was unconscious of the passing time. This was what he had to do, even if only for a couple hours in the evening. It was the only way that he had to balance the tedious job at Bendix. Losing himself in his artwork was a blessing to Lynd, and he never betrayed this blessing.

Anyway, he saw a robin today. Spring was right around the corner. And after spring came summer, and Lonely Lake. He already imagined the cry of the loons and the stone walls he would build.

Conclusion

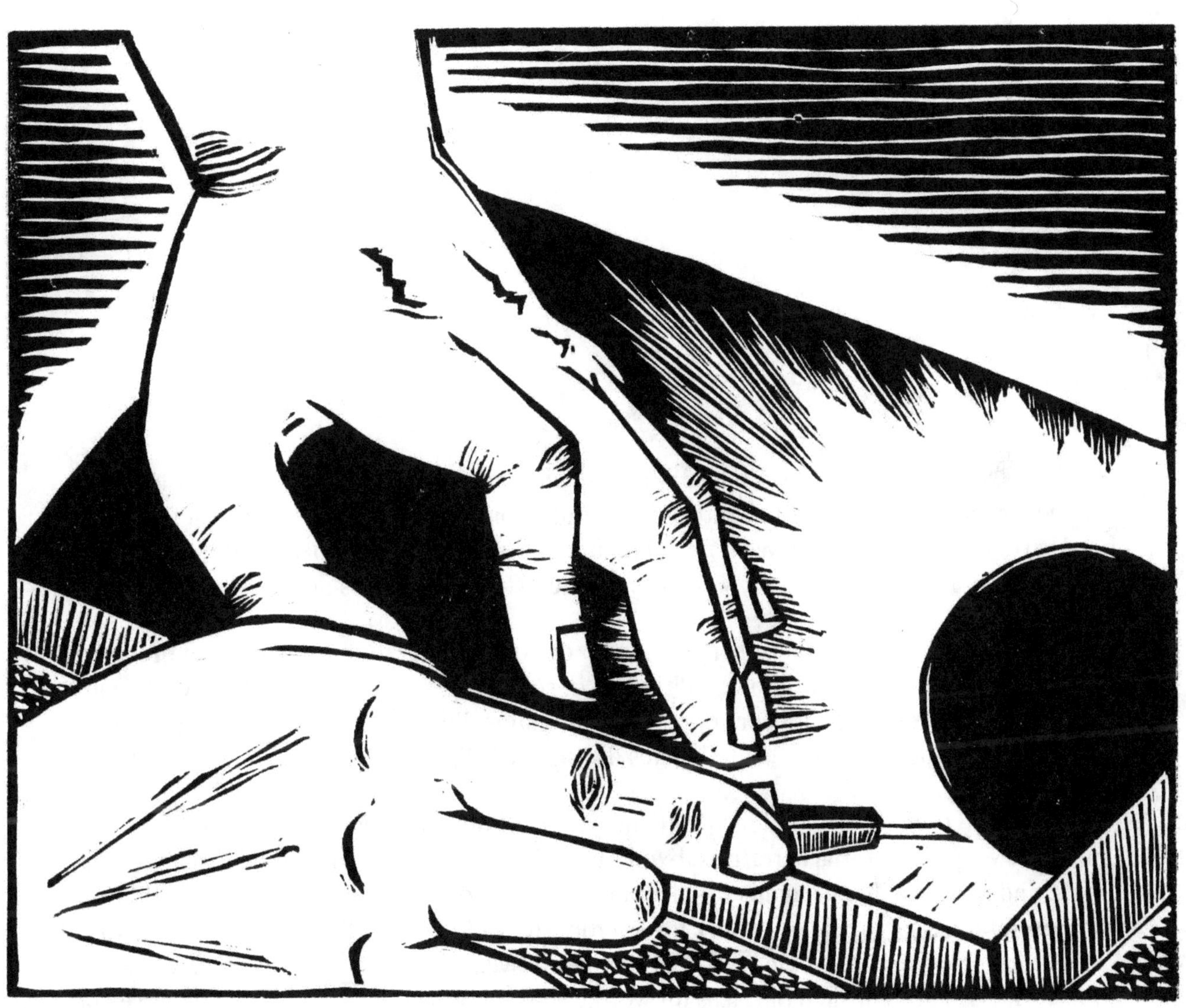

Lynd Ward was, as Michael McCurdy described him in my interview with him, a modest man. "The man was a silent man. He didn't have a lot of words to say. In fact, if he did have something to say, it was very deliberate." With this special aspect of his personality, it is not surprising to see that he was so successful with his wordless novels.

Lynd was a skillful wood engraver who discovered that the wordless novel provided him the means to convey his powerful themes of social realism. Along with Rockwell Kent, Clare Leighton, and Fritz Eichenberg, Lynd was responsible for the revival and general popularity of the woodcut in the United States during the 1930s.

Lynd took the stand-alone print and extended the plot, characters, and themes into unique sweeping pictorial narratives. Lynd's use of visually dynamic objects, consistent symbols, and thematic threads in his woodcut novels ensured first-rate storytelling. In addition to developing a pictorial vocabulary for lengthy storytelling, Lynd's experimentation with two-color printing opened the investigation of the psychological world of his characters. In this form, Lynd established the basis for wordless storytelling that is used today by artists of children's wordless picture books and wordless comics.

Finally, in his woodcut novels, Lynd documented the injustices in the American economic and social system during the Depression era. Ironically, the social ills Lynd displayed in his woodcut novels seventy years ago are evident in today's culture. Though not as readily visible as Depression-era soup lines, today's economic uncertainties, the breakup of the family, the shortage of traditional blue-collar jobs, and a general sense of isolation are realities, and are just as crucial as they were for Americans during the 1930s.

American artists like Paul Cadmus and Peter Blume were just as politically active as Lynd during the 1930s, but beyond efforts to shake up the public's sense of right and wrong, Lynd's achievement as a storyteller in pictures cannot be matched.

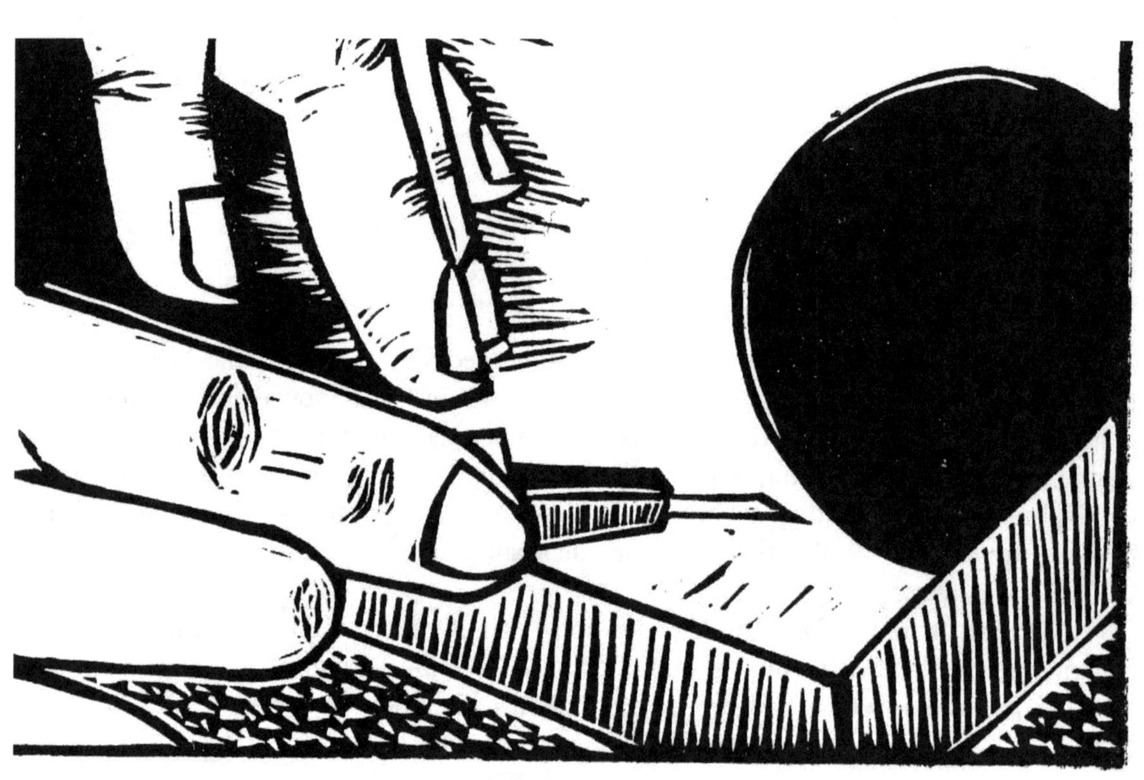

When I look at the lives of Lynd Ward, his father Harry, and his wife May, what comes to mind is a passage from Arthur Symons' *The Symbolist Movement in Literature,* when he describes the fact that we all avoid unpleasant thoughts of our own death.

> And so there is a great, silent conspiracy between us to forget death; all our lives are spent in busily forgetting death. That is why we are active about so many things which we know to be unimportant; why we are so afraid of solitude, and so thankful for the company of our fellow-creatures. Allowing ourselves, for the most part, to be but vaguely conscious of that great suspense in which we live, we find our escape from its sterile, annihilating reality in many dreams, in religion, passion, art; each a forgetfulness, each a symbol of creation; religion being the creation of a new heaven, passion the creation of a new earth, and art, in its mingling of heaven and earth, the creation of heaven out of earth. Each is a kind of sublime selfishness, the saint, the lover, and the artist having each an incommunicable ecstasy which he esteems as his ultimate attainment; however, in his lower moments, he may serve God in action, or do the will of his mistress, or minister to men by showing them a little beauty. But it is, before all things, an escape, and the prophets who have redeemed the world, and the artists who have made the world beautiful, and the lovers who have quickened the pulses of the world, have really, whether they knew it or not, been fleeing from the certainty of one thought: that we have, all of us, only our one day; and from the dread of that other thought: that the day, however used, must after all be wasted.

Symons goes on to state that this knowledge "is the hardest path to walk in, where you are told only, walk well; it is perhaps the only counsel of perfection which can ever really mean much to the artist."

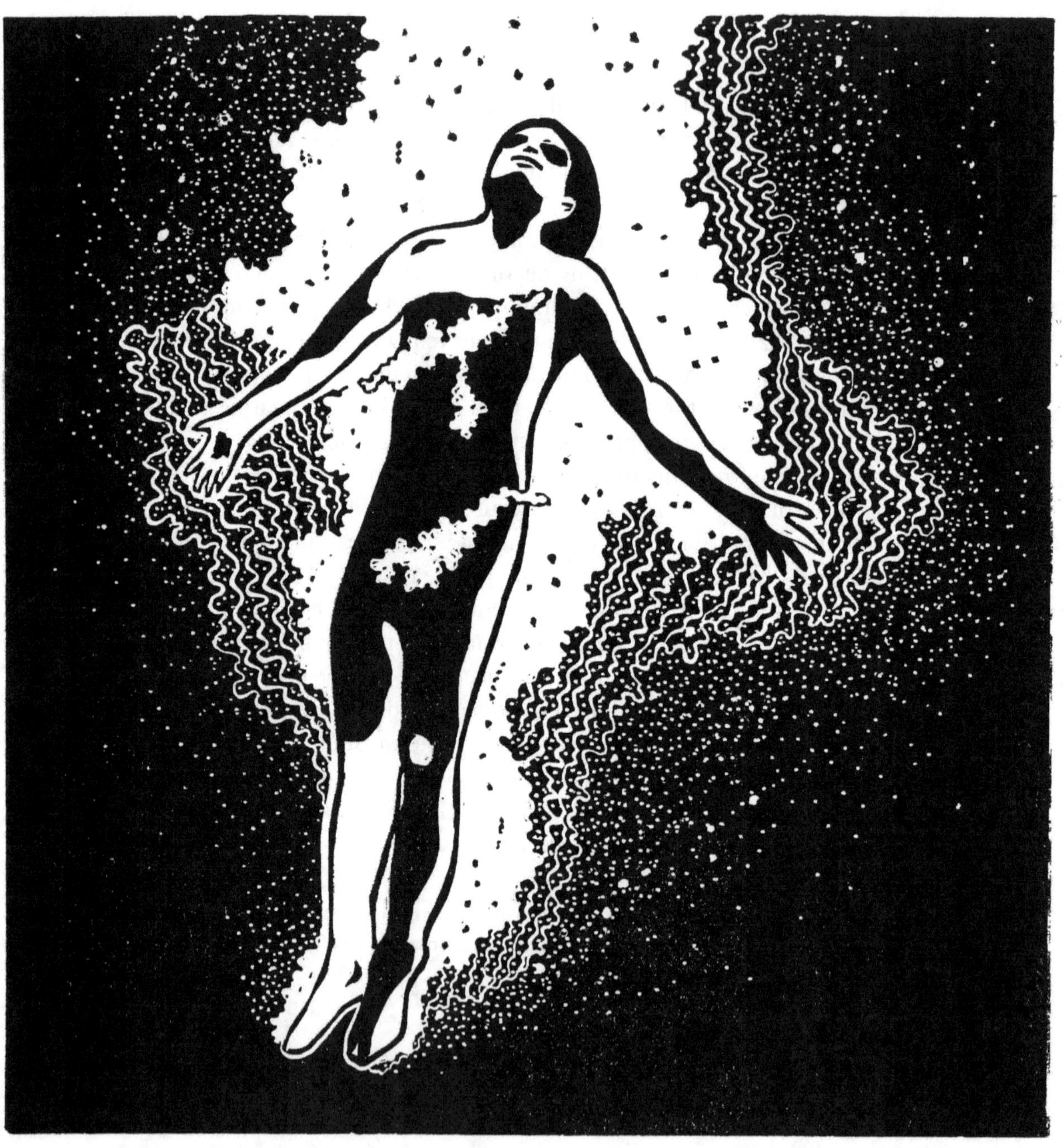

On a personal note, I had the privilege to visit Lonely Lake in July 2001 with Ward's two daughters and their families. One morning, with an exceptional stillness on the lake, I stood on the boat dock at Nanda Ward's cabin. The lake was so calm that it reflected the puffy clouds like a mirror. I took off my clothes and slipped down off the dock into the tranquility of the moment, entered the water quietly, careful not to disturb the serenity that I felt at that moment. I dove down under the water, and recalling that Lynd's ashes were floating in the lake, I took a quick sip of the water and rose to the surface, feeling as though I had found the closure I needed after my research on Lynd Ward. Since the water reflected the clouds so dramatically, I felt as though I was floating on the clouds in the heavens.

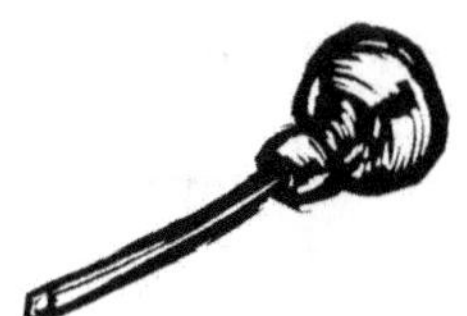

David A. Beronä was a historian of woodcut novels and wordless comics who published and presented papers widely on wordless books. He is the author of *Wordless Books: The Original Graphic Novels*, Abrams, New York, 2008. Beronä served on the editorial board of the *International Journal of Comic Art*. He was the director of Lamson Library at Plymouth State University, New Hampshire, and visiting faculty member at the Center for Cartoon Studies, White River Junction, Vermont.

Eric Drooker is a painter and graphic novelist. His paintings have appeared on dozens of covers of *The New Yorker*, while his graphics and street posters are a familiar site in the global street art movement. He won the American Book Award for *Flood! A Novel in Pictures*, soon followed by *Blood Song*, and *Howl: A Graphic Novel.* He was animation designer for the film, *Howl.*

Several years ago David A. Beronä and I talked about illustrating his fictionalized life of Lynd Ward. Other projects got in the way. But when David became ill in 2014 I asked a group of artists to create woodcut or linoleum cut prints to bring his book to completion. David did not live to see the final results of this collaboration but he was able to see the pieces as they came together. All of us felt great love and respect for David for his scholarship of woodcut novels, his enthusiasm for contemporary artwork and his support for us as individual artists.

Art Hazelwood

The artists include: **Olivier Deprez, Jules Remedios Faye, Drew Grasso, Art Hazelwood, Frances Jetter, Billy Simms, Kurt Brian Webb.**

www.ingramcontent.com/pod-product-compliance
Lightning Source LLC
LaVergne TN
LVHW081254100826
845148LV00009B/1220

* 9 7 8 0 9 1 5 1 1 7 2 5 3 *